Stephen Hiemstra has written yet another impactful and thought-provoking book for the church. In a world where ethics and morality within the church are continuously being challenged and redefined by human thought and reason, it is refreshing to see a book that, in simple terms, provides a clear framework for recognizing genuine biblical leadership. And yet, Christian leadership is not reserved for an elect few. No, Christ requires the entirety of His church to attain Godly characteristics that reflect His attributes to a lost and dying world. We are His representatives, and how we live and conduct our lives establishes for the Lord His reputation. Here, Stephen has done a remarkable job highlighting for us what should be intuitive to every Christian filled and born again of the Holy Spirit. Thank you for speaking God's truth and providing clarity and stability for those of us who are continually seeking to become like Christ—moral and ethical leaders who live and die by God's biblical standards.

Eric Teitelman
Author and Pastor, House of David Ministries
(www.TheHouseOfDavid.org)

Stop burning rubber in your faith life! Living in Christ explores the point at which the rubber meets the road for Christians. For a car, the power from the engine transforms into motion through the tires. For a human, faith in Christ transforms into real life choices through ethics. Without a good exploration of Christian ethics, even the most powerful faith in Jesus has no way to transform into decisions that move us forward. Stephen Hiemstra's discussion of Christian ethics is like a great set of tires, providing traction for our faith. It is detailed, relevant, and current. It provides a touchstone for our own personal ethical reflection, something you will need if you want to run the race without spinning tires at the starting line.

Aaron Gordon
Pastor, First Presbyterian Church of Ponchatoula
(www.FirstPresbyterianPonchatoula.com)

Also by Stephen W. Hiemstra:

A Christian Guide to Spirituality

Called Along the Way

Everyday Prayers for Everyday People

Life in Tension

Oraciones

Prayers

Prayers of a Life in Tension

Simple Faith

Spiritual Trilogy

Una Guía Cristiana a la Espiritualidad

LIVING IN CHRIST

Almost Forgotten Winter Path

LIVING IN CHRIST

Character, Community, and Leadership

Stephen W. Hiemstra

T2Pneuma Publishers LLC
Centreville, Virginia

LIVING IN CHRIST
Character, Community, and Leadership

Copyright © 2020 Stephen W. Hiemstra. All rights reserved.
ISNI: 0000-0000-2902-8171

With the except of short excerpts used in articles and critical reviews, no part of this work may be reproduced, transmitted, or stored in any form whatsoever, printed or electronic, without prior written permission of the publisher.

T2Pneuma Publishers LLC
P.O. Box 230564, Centreville, VA 20120
http://www.T2Pneuma.com

Names: Hiemstra, Stephen Wayne, author.
Title: Living in Christ : character, community, and leadership / Stephen W. Hiemstra.
Series: Christian Spirituality
Description: Includes bibliographical references and index. | Centreville, VA: T2Pneuma Publishers LLC, 2020.
Identifiers: LCCN: 2019918746 | ISBN: 978-1-942199-26-7 (pbk.) | 978-1-942199-73-1 (epub) | 978-1-942199-98-4 (KDP)
Subjects: LCSH Spiritual life--Christianity. | Christian life. | Christian leadership. | Christian ethics. | BISAC RELIGION / Christian Living / Spiritual Growth | RELIGION / Christian Theology / Ethics
Classification: LCC BV4501.2.H 2020 | DDC 248.4--dc23

My thanks to Nathan Snow and Dennis Hollinger for helpful comments and to Sarah Hamaker for her thorough editing.

All Scripture quotations, unless otherwise indicated, are taken from The Holy Bible, English Standard Version, Copyright © 2000; 2001 by Crossway Bibles, a division of Good News Publishers. Used by permission. All rights reserved.

Cover art: "Runner " by Steve Kuzma (www.SteveKuzma.com). Used by Permission.
Cover and layout designed by SWH

CONTENTS

TITLE PAGE.. iii
COPYRIGHT PAGE... iv
FOREWORD... vii
PREFACE... xvii

INTRODUCTION
Living Expectantly.. 2
Character.. 7
Community.. 12
Leadership.. 18
Chapter Notes... 25

ETHICAL CONCEPTS
From Mere Isness to Maturity... 28
Ethics Defined... 32
Identity, Duty, and Planning... 39
Tradeoffs, Desires, and Temptations.................................. 46
Problem of Boundaries.. 50
Humility and Family Ethics... 55
Ministerial Ethics.. 61
Presuppositional Ethics.. 68
Risk Takers for Christ.. 75

CHARACTER
Ethical Perspective.. 80
Interpreting Life... 83
Learning to Tack.. 88
Anger and Murder.. 92
Spiritual Disciplines.. 95
The Value of Life.. 99
Ninevites... 102
Creation Living.. 108
Sunshine and Exercise.. 113
Transcendence and Identity... 118

COMMUNITY
Moses' Call..126
Interpretative Community................................. 128
Cultural Context... 131
Language.. 140
Dialogue..146
Church and State Up Until the Reformation............ 151
Church and State Since the Reformation................. 156
Hidden Ministries...166
Downward Mobility..173
A Worshipping Community............................... 178

LEADERSHIP
Self-Care..184
Holiness..190
Generational Reach... 196
Beyond Default Settings..................................... 200
Managing Change...205
Christian Distinctives....................................... 210
Show, Don't Tell... 214
From the Heart..218

SPECIAL ISSUES
Authentic Grief..223
Unpaid Work...228
A Sheep Story.. 235
Misplaced Affections.. 239
Covered and Healed...245

CONCLUSION
Wrapping Up...250
Summary... 256
Finding Closure..259

REFERENCES... 265
SCRIPTURAL INDEX... 289
ABOUT... 293

FOREWORD

Rollin A. Van Broekhoven

JD, LLM, DPhil, DLitt.

Manassas, Virginia

British sociologist and author, Os Guinness, in his 2013 book, *The Global Public Square: Religious Freedom and the Making of the World Safe for Diversity*, wrote: "We are now seven billion people jostling together on our tiny planet earth." He then asks:

> How do we live with our deepest differences, especially those differences that are religious and ideological, and especially when those differences concern matters of our public life? How do we create a global public square and make the world safe for diversity?

Three questions arise. First, do we believe in the measureless dignity and worth of each of us? Second, do we know how to live with our differences? And three, how are we to settle our differences in public life through persuasion rather than force, intimidation, and violence, in view of media, technology, and a global resurgence of religion. He then states: "Indispensable to solving these challenges is the extension of soul freedom for all." Soul freedom means that inviolable freedom of thought, conscience, religion and belief that alone does full justice to the dictates of our humanity. It expresses human dignity; it promotes universal freedom and justice; it fosters healthy giving, caring, peaceful and stable societies as bulwarks against abuses of power and oppression of human dignity.

In his book, *The Abolition of Man: How Education Develops Man's Sense of Morality*, C. S. Lewis wrote that when we say something important, we are actually only expressing something about our own feelings. Until modern times, all humanity believed to be such that certain emotional reactions could be either congruous or incongruous to the universe—believed that objects did not merely receive, but could merit our approval or disapproval, our reverence or our content.

Apologist and evangelist, Ravi Zacharias (2011) tells the story of two Australian sailors on shore leave in London. They spent the night drinking at a local pub. When they left the pub and went out into London fog, they became disoriented and could not find their way back to the ship.

A highly decorated senior British naval officer

happened by in the fog and they asked him: "Mate, can you help us get back to our ship?"

Insulted by their approach, he asked them: "Do you know who I am?"

At which point, sailors said: "Mate, we are in a mess now, we don't know where we are and this bloke doesn't know who he is!"

This story parallels the deeper challenges facing the Western world today. We have lost track of where we are in human history and our ignorance lays bare the underlying challenges to identity, nature, and law faced equally in the East and the West.

The need for clear thinking about worldviews and how they affect our ethics has never been greater. The absence of ethics is imbedded into every sector of society, government, industry, education, and even the church. I became interested in both of these topics about forty years ago, when I only knew my Christian heritage. I draw my philosophy of law mostly from the Holy Scriptures, and St. Thomas Aquinas. When other writers proudly proclaim themselves as Kantian, Hegelians, Marxist, Benthamites, Platonists, Confucianists, Darwinians, Spinozists, and so on, why should I be ashamed to be a Christian philosopher of law?

Few truly think about worldviews, how they affect ethics, and that a priori Truth exists. Even fewer think of ethics in metaphysical (what is reality and what is our place in reality), epistemological (how we know what we think we know), and axiological terms (value theory and theories of obligation). As a lawyer, judge, and law professor thinking about law, why I should bring such things as theology, philosophy, ethics, sociology, and economic theories into the mix?

A worldview begins with wonder. Does order exist in the universe and, if so, what should we think about it? How do our values, attitudes, and purposes of life influence our activities? Although Dr. Hiemstra addressed metaphysics and epistemology in other books, he also weaves them into his current discussion of ethics. While he does not address value theory and theories of obligation directly, they are clearly implied.

Metaphysically, God is the ultimate reality and our place in that reality is our relationship to Him. Genesis 1:1 states: "In the beginning, God create the heaven and the earth." This is not a philosophical argument for the existence of God or for His creative activities. Then, God said:

> Let us make man in our image, after our likeness. And let them have dominion over the fish of the sea and over the birds of the heavens and over the livestock and over all the earth and over every creeping thing that creeps on the earth. (Gen 1:26)

This image portrays human beings concretely as personal, rational, and moral, not philosophically abstract. In Genesis 3, we read also of human moral consciousness, for when Adam and Eve disobeyed God's command, their eyes were open and they were ashamed, hiding from God. This is the metaphysical foundation for our ethics.

This is how metaphysics and epistemology fit together. If all answers to metaphysics questions about reality are naturalistic or materialistic, then they are based on sense perception and data collection. In this way, metaphysics points to epistemology and vice versa.

Epistemology asks four basic questions:

1. Where does knowledge originate?

2. What is the nature of knowledge? Is it objective or subjective?

3. How is knowledge acquired and tested?

4. What are the limits of knowledge.

One way to think about epistemology is to picture the noetic structure of the brain as a spider web. Looking at the web, spokes come from the outer structure to the center held together by circles that represent all that you have heard, experienced, and learned in your lifetime. The innermost circles are the control beliefs that give sense and coherence to what you have heard, experienced, or learned over a lifetime that order the world and your place in it.

For a Christian, the innermost circle is the presupposition that God exists, that He created the universe and all that exists therein, and that He created men and women in His image. We may not prove our control beliefs, but they are necessary to make sense of life and the world, including our ethics.

The Psalmist writes:

> The heavens declare the glory of God, and the sky above proclaims his handiwork. Day to day pours out speech, and night to night reveals knowledge . . . The law of the LORD is perfect, reviving the soul; the testimony of the LORD is sure, making wise the simple; the precepts of the LORD are right, rejoicing the heart; the commandment of the LORD is

pure, enlightening the eyes (Ps 19:1–2, 7–8)
The Christian understanding of creation connects the Works of God to the Being of God. Creation and redemption are not merely interconnected with the economy of salvation; they embody the character of God. These tie both the epistemological and axiological elements together.

We recognize two sorts of beliefs: Mediated beliefs reached from other beliefs and unmediated beliefs adopted without reference to other beliefs. Justification expresses the idea that epistemology is normative. A belief may be justified because it results from a reliable process or provides a coherent answer. Logic requires that our answer adhere to the law of noncontradiction. In other words, opposite claims cannot both be true.

The naturalist argues for a scientific explanation of reality that relies primarily on sight, hearing, and feeling with the natural senses. Their reductionistic reality is limited to causal observations and experiences with the senses within the closed system of time and space. The God of the Bible and moral demands will never make sense to this person because they are not sense perceptions.

By contrast, a rationalist argues that as humans we participate in two domains: The immaterial and universal "real" and the material "real." The rationalist view is open to understanding the God of the Bible and moral demands that confound the naturalist.

Consequently, two basic theories of knowledge exist. In the first, our understanding of what is real is a posteriori based on experience and the data collected. The second is idealism where the mind accepts a priori ideas that are self-evident and intuitively embraced.

Axiology is value theory and theories of obligation and morality. Two kinds of values exist: Intrinsic values that are valuable in and of themselves and extrinsic or instrumental values that depend on other values. Axiology asks: What ultimate value or summon bonum directs our lives? Many instrumental values may increase your love, goodness, happiness, pleasure, wealth, justice, common good, or love, but intrinsic values are rare.

In the Bible, the summon bonum is clearly stated: "You shall love the LORD your God with all your heart and with all your soul and with all your might." (Deut 6:5) Jesus restates this verse as: "You shall love the Lord your God with all your heart and with all your soul and with all your mind." (Matt 22:37) In discussing the summon bonum, Dr. Hiemstra writes: "Christian ethics requires that we strive in our daily walk to make Christ our number-one priority." Other values are instrumental to this ultimate value.

With this theory of value, two theories of obligation follow: Deontology and consequentialism. Three questions arise. First, what ought I to do? Second, are moral rules and actions right or wrong of themselves? Third, are the consequences of an act or rule relevant to the rightness or wrongness of the act or rule?

This third question separates deontology from consequentialism. Deontology identifies the ethical, or right or wrong, in and of itself without regard to the consequences. Consequentialism defines what is ethical, or right or wrong, purely on the basis of the consequences that flow from the act or rule.

In his examples, Dr. Hiemstra, touches on the "creation mandate" before moving to the Ten Commandments. This suggests that ethics consistently starts with the "creation mandate," the proceeds through the history of Israel, Mosaic law, the prophets, the teachings of Jesus, and ultimately the writings of the apostles, especially the apostle Paul.

Although this foreword is more theoretical than Dr. Hiemstra's book, it sets a context for what follows in *Living in Christ*. I encourage readers to engage our culture and not limit themselves to the church. While ethics can be theoretical and philosophical, it is also relevant to issues of abortion, bioethics, medical ethics, same-sex relationships, business ethics, and daily living. Many who are not followers of Jesus may believe and act in accordance with what Dr. Hiemstra has written without the summon bonum, which characterizes our life in Christ.

PREFACE

Do you not know that in a race all the runners run,
but only one receives the prize?
So run that you may obtain it.
(1 Cor 9:24)

The Christian walk begins with spiritual rebirth (John 3:3). On the Day of Pentecost, the Apostle Peter described rebirth for adult believers in these terms: "Repent and be baptized every one of you in the name of Jesus Christ for the forgiveness of your sins, and you will receive the gift of the Holy Spirit." (Acts 2:38) Here rebirth is a lifelong transition that starts with repentance, belief in the resurrection of Christ, and baptism. It then proceeds under the mentorship of the Holy Spirit.

Every journey has a destination. As in the Parable of the Talents, Christians live in anticipation of Christ's return and to hear the words:

> Well done, good and faithful servant. You have been faithful over a little; I will set you over much. Enter into the joy of your master. (Matt 25:21)

In the power of the Holy Spirit, Christian ethics requires modeling ourselves after Christ, striving to advance the Kingdom, and living in the hope of Christ's return in glory. In Christ, we live joyfully knowing who we serve and how the story ends.

Although we often interpret the Gospel as individuals, we live in a community modeled after a Triune God—Father, Son, and Holy Spirit—who lives in perfect, eternal harmony. We are never alone in coming to faith, working out our gifts as we prosper in faith, and living in anticipation of Christ's return. Being created in the image of a perfect and holy God, God himself models in Christ what it means to be good, to be emotionally stable, and to judge rightly. Our hearts and minds are wholly integrated. Because we live in a community that values integration, we strive together to perfect our characters and our talents, respecting spiritual boundaries provided by God himself.

Part of our own maturation process is learning to live responsibly in community and to offer leadership in our families, in the community of faith, and in the wider society. Christian leadership is rooted in humility that leaves room in our personal and corporate lives for God's intervention. For this reason, inner strength, not physical strength, exemplifies the Christian leader because self-confident people are the ones who take up the wash-basin and follow Christ (John 13:3–15).

Ethics is an important component of Christian spirituality. A complete spirituality addresses each of the four questions typically posed in philosophy:

1. Metaphysics—who is God?
2. Anthropology—who are we?
3. Epistemology—how do we know?
4. Ethics—what do we do about it? (Kreeft 2007, 6)

My first two books—*A Christian Guide to Spirituality* and *Life in Tension*—address the metaphysical question. My third book—*Called Along the Way*—explores the anthropological question in the first person. My fourth book, *Simple Faith*, examined the epistemological question. In *Living in Christ*, I explore the ethics question, writing not as one with specialized training in philosophy, but as someone focused on Christian spirituality—Christian living. How do we live out our faith?

In *Living in Christ*, I focus on explaining, not

justifying, Christian ethics. At a time and in a place where people scoff at developing a theological understanding of their faith and refuse to teach Christian morality, ethics is almost a lost art. At the heart of the ethical dilemma is a tension between theological principles that can only be resolved the guidance of the Holy Spirit. For example, how do you practice forgiveness for sinners who refuse to confess their sin and force you to bear its consequences? In this context, ethics is less a philosophical discipline that a recognition of our own limitations as Christians and the need for divine intervention.

Ethical thought and action always involve interpretation under the guidance of the Holy Spirit. It is thus ironic that a book on Christian living should have an outward focus on God rather than an inward focus on what to do and not do. This interpretative element colors how we view character formation, the community of faith, leadership, and the many special issues that arise in daily life.

Soli Deo Gloria.

INTRODUCTION

Christian ethics starts with God in whose image we are created. Creation begins with birth and continues as we mature. Our character matures shaped by the example of Christ under the mentorship of the Holy Spirit through the family and the church. Christians reach full maturity once they able to mentor others.

Living Expectantly

*M*oral confusion pervades postmodern culture. Furthermore, it threatens our persons and our way of life. As we struggle to make sense of life and survive in a sinful world, conversations about Christian morality always begins with God.

Normalization of Drugs

Whenever moral confusion is discussed, our minds gravitate towards immoral sexual activity. However, the normalization of drug use highlights this confusion more clearly. The federal government recently reported:

> In 2014, 27.0 million people aged 12 or older used an illicit drug in the past 30 days, which corresponds to about 1 in 10 Americans (10.2 percent). This percentage in 2014 was higher than those in every year from 2002 through 2013. (CBHSQ 2015, 1)

How does the body politic respond to this serious social crisis? Because most drug use involves marijuana, Alaska, California, Colorado, Maine, Massachusetts, Nevada, Oregon, Vermont, and Washington, DC have as of June 2019 legalized recreational use of marijuana.[1] This response suggests that in spite of the negative medical impacts of marijuana use and the crime commonly associated with drug use, these states have legalized use.

Negative Impacts of Drugs

While we might debate the morality of consuming illegal drugs, the criminal activity associated with providing these substances have devastated communities throughout Central American and has contributed to historically high levels of illegal immigration into the United States in recent decades (Whelan 2018). The inability of many young people to pass random drug tests has made it difficult for American companies, especially defense contractors, to recruit employees. The flip side of this recruiting problem is that many Americans have systematically precluded themselves from a job in their chosen field or in their local community because of drug use.

Why the moral concern about drug use? Drug use impairs mental concentration—including moral discernment—and is often associated with criminal activity, depression, and suicide. Record drug use is also associated with a thirty-year high in suicides (Tavernise 2016). Reinforcing this observation, alcohol intoxication is reported in about half of all suicides (Mason 2014, 34).

Christian Ethics

Christian ethics starts with God in whose image we are created (Gen 1:27). In the Old Testament, God interacts with his people primarily through the cutting of covenants. After a second giving of the Ten Commandments, God reveals his character to Moses:

> The LORD passed before him and proclaimed, The LORD, the LORD, a God merciful and gracious, slow to anger, and abounding in steadfast love and faithfulness. (Exod 34:6)

God's character provides a context for interpreting the Ten Commandments in the Book of Exodus, but it also outlines a template for ethical behavior. Jesus endorses this image-ethic in the Lord's Prayer when he prays: "Your kingdom come, your will be done, on earth as it is in heaven." (Matt 6:10) The Apostle Paul says directly to "be imitators of God." (Eph 5:1) In God's image, we are given both rational boundaries (commandments) and behavioral boundaries (God's character traits).

Later in Matthew, Jesus tells us to love God and neighbor (Matt 22:36–40). We embody this love first by imitating God's ethical character, then by sharing this character with our neighbor. Remember that mercy, grace, patience, love, and faithfulness all require an object. The obvious object here is our neighbor. God is a suitable object of our love, but not our grace or mercy because he is sinless and the source of our inspiration.

Jesus Christ is the vine and we are the branches. Christ is our ethical role model on whom we must depend. Through the power and guidance of the Holy Spirit, we can interpret life's alternatives knowing that we remain in Christ.

Ethics and Judgment

Circling back to the moral confusion in postmodern culture, Christians are often accused of being judgmental. But judgment and discernment differ. As Christians, we discern that most immoral behavior is also risky, suggesting a direct link with how we were created.

Risk is an expected loss. Moral behavior works like the premium on an insurance policy that protects us from a knowable and avoidable loss. Most people hate paying insurance premiums until they experience a loss for themselves and need the insurance.

If we discern that a behavior places someone at risk

of a loss, we should inform them humbly of our insight, be it from scripture or life experience, and pray that they will not incur the loss or, should it be incurred, that they will turn to God. Prayer leaves room for God's sovereign grace, and, if we are humble about discussing the matter, we may also gain the confidence of that person in dealing with future issues.

Christian Distinctive

What sets Christians apart from others, especially secular people, is that we live, not expecting death, but Christ's return. Life is not a risk; it is an opportunity to prepare for our ultimate homecoming. We live life taking chances for the kingdom and leaving room for joy, because we know the end of the story is in Christ.

Character

> *You did not choose me, but I chose you and appointed you that you should go and bear fruit.*
> (John 15:16)

What is a Christian?

Is a Christian someone who has been baptized and confirmed or is it someone who draws closer to Christ with each passing day? The formalities of baptism and confirmation mark the institutional church while the relational act of drawing closer to Christ is often associated with the pietist movement (Gehrz and Pattie 2017). Mission circles actively debate this question, in part, because in many nations around the world, church membership can bring persecution, arrest, and even death.

The Ancient Church

For scripture and for the ancient church, the tension between formality and relationship posed a false dichotomy. Jesus invited his disciples into relationship a long time before the church even existed:

> As Jesus passed on from there, he saw a man

called Matthew sitting at the tax booth, and he said to him, follow me. And he rose and followed him. (Matt 9:9)

Still, even Jesus insisted on some formalities:

> So everyone who acknowledges me before men, I also will acknowledge before my father who is in heaven, but whoever denies me before men, I also will deny before my father who is in heaven. (Matt 10:32–33)

Later the church's new member instruction could take years before a new believer underwent baptism, suggesting that baptism was more than a mere formality. Clearly, the early church took discipling seriously and engaged the inner life of the disciple beyond the reciting of a few Bible verses and a confessional statement.

Character Versus Personality

In his book, *Losing Our Virtue*, David Wells makes a distinction between character, which arises from our inner life and virtues, and personality, which focuses on outward appearances. He writes:

> Today, we cultivate personality (a word almost unknown before the twentieth century) far more than we do character, and this is simply the concomitant to the way in which values have come to replace the older sense of virtue . . . Character is good or bad, while personality is attractive, forceful, or

magnetic. (Wells 1998, 96–97)

The "hollowing out of the self" began with this emphasis on exterior characteristics and is exemplified by the rise of celebrities over heroes, as found in classical literature. Wells (1998, 100) notes, citing Daniel Boorstin:

> The hero was distinguished by his achievement; the celebrity by his image or trademark. The hero created himself; the celebrity is created by the media.

The focus on external appearances and the neglect of the inner life are akin to devaluing our experience of God, even if we believe that we take faith seriously. Wells (1998, 108) observes:

> If the narcissist classically has a shrunken, fragmentary self, our culture has similarly become hollowed out and lost its core. If the narcissist covers up the emptiness by exaggerated self-importance and fantasies of power, our culture is covering up its hollowness by fads and fashions, ceaseless consuming, and the constant excitement of fresh sexual conquest.

While someone of strong moral character has no need of buzz, personality addicts live for public approval—they are the classic people pleasers. In Washington, DC, the old joke was that most dangerous place to stand is between a particular politician and the television cameras.

Looking Beyond Personality

In the midst of a culture that constantly shouts at us, it can be hard to hear the still, small voice of God. If the shouting creates a crisis atmosphere that tempts us to ignore our inner life, to abandon our walk with Christ, and to evaluate our worth by secular standards, then our culture forms our character and our number-one priority is not God, as required by the first Commandment (Exod 20:3–5). We commit idolatry when our identity lies primarily with our family, work, gender, or other things.

Identity is critical to Christian ethical practice. Just like firefighters who run into burning buildings, not away from them, our identities shape our actions. This makes character formation a priority for Christian families and the church.

Number-One Priority

Jesus constantly talked about the heart and loving the right things—his way of talking about character formation and an allusion to the first Commandment—as we read:

> The good person out of the good treasure of his heart produces good, and the evil person out of his evil treasure produces evil, for

> out of the abundance of the heart his mouth speaks. (Luke 6:45)

For the Hebrew, heart and mind are undivided, components of a unified whole, as we are reminded in the Shema, the Jewish Daily Prayer, "You shall love the LORD your God with all your heart and with all your soul and with all your might," (Deut 6:5) which Jesus repeats in his Greatest Commandment discourse (Matt 22:36–40). Implicit in this discussion of heart and mind is acting out with our hands what we know to be true in our hearts and minds (Hollinger 2005, 145–146).

If we act out of our identity, then obviously Christian ethics requires that we strive in our daily walk to make Christ our number-one priority.

Community

> *Behold, how good and pleasant it is*
> *when brothers and sisters dwell in unity!*
> *(Ps 133:1)*

The word for church commonly used in the New Testament in Greek literally means the called out ones (e.g. Jas 5:14). The Apostle Paul writes:

> To the church of God that is in Corinth, to those sanctified in Christ Jesus, called to be saints together with all those who in every place call upon the name of our Lord Jesus Christ, both their Lord and ours. (1 Cor 1:2)

Bonhoeffer (1995, 226) builds on this idea when he writes: "The preaching of the Church and the administration of the sacraments is the place where Jesus Christ is present." Bonhoeffer's statement echoes Christ's own words (e.g. John 6:56).

Priesthood of All Believers

The idea of the called-out ones today evokes the image of a seminary, where men and women called to professional ministry receive formal training. But every member of the church is called to faith and ministry. As with Abraham, we are blessed to be a blessing to others (Gen 12:1–3). We are all priests serving under our great high priest, Jesus Christ, and are able to approach God through him (Heb 7:25).

Although the doctrine of the priesthood of all believers is often interpreted narrowly to mean that church members should invite their neighbors and friends to church, the Apostle Peter links this priestly function specifically to sanctification:

> So put away all malice and all deceit and hypocrisy and envy and all slander . . . As you come to him, a living stone rejected by men but in the sight of God chosen and precious, you yourselves like living stones are being built up as a spiritual house, to be a holy priesthood, to offer spiritual sacrifices acceptable to God through Jesus Christ. (1 Pet 2:1–5)

Note how these verses begin with a call to purity. Is it any wonder that scripture likens the church to a marriage?

Marriage and the Scripture

The Bible begins and ends with a marriage, which suggests marriage is God's idea, not ours (Keller 2011, 13).

Beginning in the Book of Genesis, we see a couple, Adam and Eve, who are just made for each other and whose relationship is more important than the man's relationship with his family (Gen 2:24). That a man's wife was more important than his family of origin was unthinkable in the Ancient Near East where siblings, not spouses, were one's closest confidants (Hellerman 2001, 36).

Ending in the Book of Revelation, an angel informs us: "Blessed are those who are invited to the marriage supper of the Lamb." (Rev 19:9) The church, betrothed to Christ on earth, is finally married to Christ in heaven. Revelation depicts many pictures of Christian worship in heaven with robes, trumpets, singing, prayer, visions, and processions that make the analogy between marriage and the church explicit.

Jesus treats the creation account of Adam and Eve as foundational in his teaching on divorce and remarriage. From the prospective of advocates of no-fault divorce, he ignores the Law of Moses that admits exceptions in divorce. If God instituted marriage in creation, then divorce is obviously not divinely sanctioned. More importantly, marriage ceases to form us if it only survives on sunny days.

The Formative Characteristics of Marriage

In what ways are the church's relationship with Christ analogous to marriage?

In his comments on mixed faith marriages, the Apostle Paul highlights the formative character of marriage. He states, for example, that the believing spouse renders the whole marriage holy for the children (1 Cor 7:12–14). Paul also sees marriage as a witnessing opportunity:

> For how do you know, wife, whether you will save your husband? Or how do you know, husband, whether you will save your wife? (1 Cor 7:16)

In other words, Paul clearly sees marriage possessing a sacrificial component mirroring Christ's own sacrifice.

If marriage is formative, how does it draw us closer to God? At least three examples can be cited.

First, God instituted marriage and commissioned marriage with a blessing and mandate: "Be fruitful and multiply and fill the earth and subdue it, and have dominion." (Gen 1:28) God created marriage, blessed it, and said it was good—obeying God draws us closer to him.

Second, marriage starts with an unconditional promise. God is the eternal promise keeper. In marriage we imitate our creator. Making and keeping good promises—even when it hurts—transforms us and draws us closer to God.

Third, marriage makes us accountable. Our spouses know us in the biblical (covenantal) way! Our weaknesses and sin affect our spouses and they tell us. We sin less, in part, because our spouses make us more aware of our sin—a sanctification process that forms us—even if we are not believers! Part of this process is to learn reconciliation skills by practicing them daily. As the Apostle Paul wrote: "And whatever you do, in word or deed, do everything in the name of the Lord Jesus, giving thanks to God the Father through him." (Col 3:17)

God instituted marriage even before he instituted the nation of Israel or sent his son to die on the cross. God is not irrational. He knows that the biggest beneficiaries of marriage are our children. He loves them as much as he loves us and as Christians we are all God's children.

Formation of Character in Community

Just like marriage, our Christian character is formed

in relationship. Our first relationship in life is with our families. In faith, our relationship is with each of the three members of the Trinity—Father, Son, and Holy Spirit. Reinforcing these other relationships is our relationship with the church. Our Christian identity develops out of these relationships and informs how we act.

The postmodern tendency is to down play the importance of Christian formation, especially in leadership, because of a deficient doctrine of sin and neglect of the heart. The New Testament treats the heart as a shorthand for the whole person—heart, mind, and soul. Sin begins in the heart and emanates into action. Acting out sin, in turn, pollutes the heart and mind making future sin more likely, which is why the Bible treats sin as an act of rebellion. This polluting characteristic of sin explains why we must remain vigilant in pursuing our Christian formation.

Formed as we are in Christian relationships, our ethics arise from faith, family, and community of faith. As we mature in our faith, we naturally assume a leadership role in each of these domains.

Leadership

> *Then he poured water into a basin and began to wash the disciples' feet and to wipe them with the towel that was wrapped around him.*
> (John 13:5)

The image of a sovereign, creator God is never more clearly reflected than in leadership. In its purest form, Christian leadership displays the kingly, priestly, and prophetic characteristics of the Messiah, revealing its origin in the godhead and formation in the community of faith. It is sovereign in being free to create; spiritual in embodying unseen power; and Christlike in its sacrificial character. Christian leadership never strays far from the cross.

What is Leadership?

In scripture, we see many images of leadership, but no clear definition. One definition of Christian leadership is:

> Good leaders are fervent disciples of Jesus Christ, gifted by the Holy Spirit, with a passion to bring glory to God. They use

their gifts of leadership by taking initiative to focus, harmonize, and enhance the gifts of others for the sake of developing people and cultivating the kingdom of God. (Plueddemann 2009, 15)

It is helpful to identify the unique role of leaders in decisions.

Role of Leaders

The scientific method is a decision tool often employed in science and management. The method consists of these steps:

1. Felt need
2. Problem definition
3. Observation
4. Analysis
5. Decision
6. Action
7. Responsibility learning.[2]

In the problem definition step, a hypothesis is formed out of a felt need. Observations about this hypothesis are collected in the second step. In the third step, these observations are analyzed in view of other discoveries. In the final steps, a decision is made whether to accept or reject the hypothesis, act, and bear responsibility for the action. Here the inactive voice is used intentionally in this description to avoid presuming who undertakes each step.

Three points in the scientific method require executive action: Defining the problem, deciding, and bearing responsibility. If the problem is inconsequential, then everything can be delegated to professional managers. But, if the problem threatens the organizational existence or objectives, then executives must be involved because substantial resources are at risk.

Spiritual Leadership

Spiritual leadership is particularly important turning felt needs into problem definitions where organizational cultures are defined. Even small decisions spiritual leadership is needed for organizational success because organizations must actively learn to adapt more rapidly to a changing environment and to capture the multiplicative effect of joint action. An organization is more than the sum of its parts. When leaders humble themselves before the Triune God, even just privately, a tone of humility is set for the entire organization and they make room for God's sovereign will to act within the organization.

Timing is Crucial

A popular business book recently divided conversation about a problem into four stages: Presenting facts, telling a story, feeling, and acting. The facts provide an outline of what needs attention and why; the story organizes the facts into a hypothesis; the story evokes an emotional response; and actions follow from this response. Once emotions take over a discussion, actions get locked in. The key point in influencing an organizational decision process therefore arises as people begin to tell stories about presumed facts (Patterson and others 2012, 3–13).

A crucial conversation arises when stakes are high, opinions vary, and emotions run strong. Responses to these white-knock conversations include: Avoidance, handled poorly, and handled well. Avoidance occurs when a leader announces a course of action that is poorly thought out, but no one wants to explain why it makes no sense. A well-handled response might observe that the action is inconsistent with organization objectives and offer an alternative that is consistent with stated objectives

(Patterson and others 2012, 3–13).

High-performance professionals earn their pay by telling supervisors discretely what they do not care to hear when the more typical response is silence. Organizations where employees are able and willing to engage in constructive conversations about sensitive matters respond quicker to crises, have fewer on-the-job injuries, save money, and reduce workplace bullying (Patterson and others 2012, 3–13).

Leadership Challenges

In his book, *In the Name of Jesus*, Henri Nouwen writes laconically about Christian leadership focusing on the three temptations of Christ in the desert before he starts his ministry (Matt 4:1–11). These temptations were: Be relevant (turn stones into bread), be popular (throw yourself off the temple), and be powerful (lead rather than to be led).

Jesus' first temptation was to be relevant—turn stones into bread (Nouwen 2002, 30). Writing about his experience at L'Arche—a live-in community for special needs patients—Nouwen reports his new friends had no interest in his accomplishments or his network of distinguished colleagues. He writes:

> This experience was and, in many ways, is still the most important experience of my new life, because it forced me to rediscover my true identity. These broken, wounded, and completely unpretentious people forced me to let go of my relevant self—the self that can do things, show things, prove things, build things—and forced me to reclaim that unadorned self in which I am completely vulnerable, open to receive and give love regardless of any accomplishments. (Nouwen 2002, 28)

If the degrees, titles, and robes are stripped away, who are you really?

Jesus' second temptation was to do something spectacular to draw attention to himself (Nouwen 2002, 53). The Gospel of Matthew records it this way:

> If you are the Son of God, throw yourself down, for it is written, He will command his angels concerning you, and on their hands they will bear you up, lest you strike your foot against a stone. (Matt 4:6)

Jesus responds, saying: "You shall not put the Lord your God to the test." (Matt 4:7) For Nouwen, the temptation to engage in heroic leadership is blunted by ministering in teams and, as a member of the L'Arche community, the need to bring along a companion from the community when he was asked to speak (Nouwen 2002, 58–59).

The third temptation of Jesus was to be powerful (Nouwen 2002, 75). He observes: "It seems easier to be God than to love God, easier to control people than to love people, easier to own life than to love life." (Nouwen 2002, 78) After re-commissioning Peter, Jesus prophesies his death:

> Truly, truly, I say to you, when you were young, you used to dress yourself and walk wherever you wanted, but when you are old, you will stretch out your hands, and another will dress you and carry you where you do not want to go. (John 21:18)

Whether we like it or not as Christian leaders, we frequently find ourselves being led. Nouwen (2002, 88) sees theological reflection as the primary antidote to the temptation to be powerful.

Chapter Notes

1. https://en.wikipedia.org/wiki/Decriminalization_of_non-medical_cannabis_in_the_United_States.

2. In class, unlike his book, Johnson (1986, 15) add a felt need as the first step following Dewey (1997).

ETHICAL CONCEPTS

Ethics is often equated with law, but law provides only general boundaries to our actions. Who we are, our influences, and our aspirations subtly shape our actions, often without our conscious awareness. This subtly links our character to our community and molds the kind of leaders that we become. It also makes it difficult to define ethics outside the bounds of community, like the faith community.

From Mere Isness to Maturity

> *The earth was without form and void, and darkness was over the face of the deep. And the Spirit of God was hovering over the face of the waters. (Gen 1:2)*

How do we know that we exist?

In my memoir, *Called Along the Way*, I recount a childhood dream:

> As a child, a dream returned to me over and over where I felt suspended, neither awake or asleep, but paralyzed as if lost in time and place. Everything was fuzzy: neither light nor dark, hot nor cold, silent nor voiced. My limbs had a tingly feeling, like an arm that had fallen asleep or a leg that refused to support your weight. To describe it as a dream suggests that I might wake up, but this dream lingered, refusing me the opportunity to stir, as if I faced a decision. Yet, what decision? (Hiemstra 2017, 1)

Hayaski (2016) describes such childhood dreams as memories from the womb.

Existence, Maturity, and Relationship

Existence implies a change from non-existence and

our awareness of this change. When I work out, some mornings I run through my mat work with little thought about it. Other days the same routine becomes impossible, not for lack of strength but because my mind is distracted—it is as if I were watching a video of my body and lost all connection to it.

Without much thought, year ago I wondered why I was frequently depressed on Saturdays. Why Saturdays? When I stopped to think about it, I realized that after a hard week of work I was physically exhausted—I was not depressed; I was tired. Absent serious reflection, I misinterpreted my own bodily experience, confusing exhaustion with depression.

Descartes' famous dictum—Cognito ergo sum (I think therefore I am)—awareness of existence presumes physical existence and the ability to reflect on it. An eye sees the world but does not necessarily distinguish itself from the world being viewed and thoughts/words have no purpose to a singular being. A better statement is that I know that I exist because I am loved by God who exists independent of the world and of me (Kreeft 2007, 22–26).

Identity Formation

The meta narrative of scripture offers an interesting interpretation of who we are. We are created in the image of God. Almost immediately thereafter, we sin, breaking the only commandment of God—do not eat of the tree of the knowledge of good and evil (Gen 1–3). A radical act of separating ourselves from God. The rest of scripture is the story of our reconciliation with God.

This brief sketch is a coming-of-age story that describes creation, the need to establish an identity independent of our parents, and then a lifelong desire to reunite with them. Much like the Parable of the Prodigal Son (Luke 15), it is a narrative about becoming an adult.

The older son in this parable provides insight into the postmodern dilemma. The older brother never established an identity independent of his father and, as such, became a biblical example of co-dependency. He serves his father out of fear and resents both his younger brother and his father. He never attains true maturity as an adult and never learns to love his father. The older brother's failure to launch leaves him immature, bitter, and unable to function as an adult, unlike his younger brother.

Existence as a Continuum

Human existence exists in a continuum from physical being to fully formed adult. Our parents are the immediate instrument of our creation and maturity by God. Alive or dead, awake or sleep, young or old, we are created beings, but our awareness of existence comes through relationship. This awareness starts with intimacy, then grows through the tension of separation and re-establishment of intimacy in independence.

For the Christian, our existence in relationship has a qualitative aspect that defines who we are and forms the foundation for all that we do. Being created in the image of a sovereign God means that we have almost limitless room for growth into that image. Because God is good, our growth into the image has an inherently ethical trajectory. Because relationships are fragile, the need for the mentoring of the Holy Spirit through prayer, scripture, and the church is intensive and ongoing.

This is the context of Christian ethics.

Ethics Defined

> *He has told you, O man, what is good; and*
> *what does the LORD require of you*
> *but to do justice, and to love kindness, and*
> *to walk humbly with your God?*
> (Mic 6:8)

What is Christian ethics?

If ethics is the study of moral action, then Christian ethics is the study of moral action starting from faith in God.

Bonhoeffer's Ethics

Because only God can ultimately determine what is good and evil, Bonhoeffer sees ethics as originating in original sin:

> The knowledge of good and evil seems to be the aim of all ethical reflection. The first task of Christian ethics is to invalidate this knowledge. (Bonhoeffer 1976, 17)

If only God knows good and evil, then ethical knowledge shows separation from God. Our conscience originates in learned morality and offers no help, being more a measure of the ethical gap among people than closeness to God

(Bonhoeffer 1976, 17–25). This gap is the source of human shame.

Bonhoeffer sees the Pharisees of the New Testament as archetypes of human conscience, judging good and evil from a religious perspective, not from God's perspective. In reconciling us with God, Jesus allows us to return to God and know God. Jesus' problem with judging (and with the Pharisees) arises from the apostasy of original sin—knowledge of good and evil (Bonhoeffer 1976, 30–33).

Philosophical Context for Christian Ethics

In looking to Jesus Christ as our divine role model, Christian ethics is often classified as a branch of virtue ethics. One author writes:

> According to virtue ethicists, actions aren't right because of their results [e.g. consequentialism] or because they follow from some hard-and-fast rule [e.g. utilitarianism]. Rather, they are right because they would be done by someone of true virtue. This person is a moral exemplar. (Shafer-Landau 2018, 257)

Virtue ethics has a long history that presumably starts with to Aristotle's *Nicomachean Ethics*. The focus here is on practical wisdom, emotional maturity, and sound judgment rather than hard and fast rules. As King Solomon observes: "The fear of the LORD is the beginning of knowledge; fools despise wisdom and instruction." (Prov 1:7) As such, in virtue ethics the belief is that moral training, experience, and practice are required both for life and leadership (Shafer-Landau 2018, 258–261).

Still, virtue ethics focuses on the values of honor and courage, virtues of the ruling class, while Christian ethics primarily values humility.

The Ethical Dilemma

The need to study ethics arises and is unavoidable because principles often come in tension with one another. Bonhoeffer (1976, 367) cites this example:

> A teacher asks a child in front of the class whether it is true that his father often comes home drunk. It is true, but the child denies it. The teacher's question has placed him in a situation for which he is not yet prepared. He feels only that what is taking place is an unjustified interference in the order of the family and that he must oppose it.

In Bonhoeffer's example, the student is presented with an ethical dilemma and must choose between the Commandments to tell the truth (Exod 20:16) and to honor your parents (Exod 20:12). Which Commandment is more important and how do you decide?

More generally, the Ten Commandments provide theological principles outlining good and bad behavior. It is helpful to distinguish good and bad principles from right and wrong actions (Johnson and Zerbi 1973, 12). In Bonhoeffer's example, it is good for the student to tell the truth and to honor parents, but it is wrong for the teacher to pose the question about the father's drunken behavior (and embarrass the student publicly) and wrong for the student to verify it in public.

The split in the church today over how to respond to homosexual behavior poses a similar ethical dilemma—do we condemn sin or witness to the sinner? Scripture advises both courses of action (e.g. 1 Cor 5:11; Matt 28:19).

Distinguishing principles from actions helps preclude dogmatic responses to ethical dilemmas when dialogue is the preferred response.

Principal Agent Problem

A principal agent problem arises when a leader makes organizational decisions based on personal benefits rather than organizational benefits. In the Bonhoeffer example, suppose that the teacher is a sadist who derives pleasure from tormenting students. By putting the student on the spot to verify the father's drunkenness in public, the teacher derives sadistic pleasure at the risk of opening the school up to a potential lawsuit from the student's family. In doing so, the teacher's interests and the school interests deviate demonstrating a principal agent problem, a special kind of ethical dilemma facing leaders.

Sexual harassment, pedophilia, taking bribes, and narcissistic leadership are all potential manifestations of the principal agent problem. In the postmodern context, a distinguishing characteristic of an amoral organization is that leadership prosecutes principal agent problems while generally eschewing the moral failings of members and leaders.

Moral Training Not Optional

Behavioral learning starts with a simple idea: Do more activities that bring pleasure and do fewer activities that bring pain. By contrast, rational learning starts with making comparisons: Activity A brought a greater benefit than activity B, so let's do more of activity A. Such comparisons require pattern recognition and memory not required in behavioral learning. Success in implementing rational learning also requires patience that many people lack.

This simple distinction between behavioral and rational learning lies at the heart of many ethical controversies, because behavioral learning can lead to logical traps. For example, the fish that grabs every tasty worm is likely to end up the fisherman's dinner. In a study of such traps, Cross and Guyer (1980, 3–4) write:

> The central thesis of this book is that a wide variety of recognized social problems can be regarded from a third view [Not stupidity; not corruption]. Drug use, air pollution, and international conflict are all instances of what we have called social traps. Put simply, a social trap is a situation characterized by multiple but conflicting rewards. Just as an ordinary trap entices its prey with the offer of an attractive bait and then punishes it by capture . . . 'social traps' draw their victims into certain patterns of behavior with promises of immediate rewards and then confront them with [longer-term] consequences that the victim would rather avoid.

In both smoking and education, conflicts in patterns of short-term and long-term costs and benefits lead those specialized in behavioral learning into ethical dilemmas that cannot be avoided without considering the entire sequence of costs and benefits.

Most ethical teaching highlights weaknesses in behavioral learning and focuses on the need to study patterns of costs and benefits in decision-making, particularly among young people. For example, my great uncle, who owned a furniture store, often advised young employees on how to establish a budget, knowing that otherwise they would spend their entire paycheck on alcohol. In affluent America, poverty is often less a matter of the size of the paycheck than how it gets spent.

Part of the task of Christian leadership is to anticipate ethical dilemmas and take steps to avoid them.

Identity, Duty, and Planning

What motivates us to act?

We may act out of identity, duty, or planning, but many times we fail to act. Procrastination is common when our motivations are unclear or we are unprepared to decide.

Rational Decisions and Procrastination

Consider the case of shopping for toothpaste. Routinely buying a particular brand or buying the cheapest is an habitual purchase where no independent decision is made. However, your habit likely began with a thorough review of alternative brands or research that suggested the brands were equally effective in preventing cavities. The investment of time and effort on that first purchase may then have convinced you to use your current rule of thumb—buy the brand or buy the cheapest. Thirty years later, you may have forgotten the research and only remember the rule of thumb.

In this illustration, the original decision involved a rational decision, while using the resulting rule is more of a behavioral decision. Ethics focuses primarily on rational decisions, where we weigh the pros and cons of a decision before deciding. Behavioral decisions, where we simply respond to positive and negative stimuli, are not necessarily unethical, but they may cloak our motivations.

If you took up smoking in high school, for example, your habit may be closely associated with a person or experience back then with great personal meaning. Giving up smoking is hard. More generally, Miller and Rollnick (2002, 10) ask whether we are "ready, willing, and able" to change our habits, suggesting that we frequently are not ready, willing, or able.

When our habits are disrupted and we need to make a rational decision, deciding may be difficult. Rational decisions require more information, skill, and effort than behavioral decisions or simply more time than we have, which leads to procrastination. Furthermore, our previous decisions may be based on substantial investment that may be hard to walk away from. If a new decision is particularly costly, we may simply not be willing or able to set aside the old one. Giving up alcohol may, for example, require the alcoholic to walk away from old friends and make new ones, something always hard to do.

Identity and Character

We are created in the image of God, the core of our Christian identity: "So God created man in his own image, in the image of God he created him; male and female he created them." (Gen 1:27) The context here is important. We are in the first chapter of the first book in the Bible, so everything implied by this verse about what it means to be created in the image of God has to appear in the prior verses. How does the text describe God?

Consider these four attributes:

1. Verse one tells us that God is a creator who, being eternal, sovereignly stands outside time and space.

2. Verse two shows us that God can through his spirit enter into his creation.

3. Verse three describes God, having created heaven and earth, speaking to shape the form of creation beginning with light. Note the exact correspondence between what God says ("Let there be light") and what he does ("and there was light")—God is truthful, authentic.

4. Verse four tells us that God judged it to be good and he separated it from darkness—God discriminates good (light) from the not so good (darkness).

God is sovereign, authentic, and ethically minded. If God has these attributes, then as image bearers we should aspire to them too.

By contrast, some of God's traits are not likely to be emulated by his image bearers. Consider the question of God's sovereignty. For us, sovereignty could mean having the courage to commit the time and energy to make good decisions. By contrast, being all-powerful and all-knowing, God is unlikely to be reluctant or afraid of making tough decisions.

Identity motivates us particularly in our careers. Firefighters are easily identified as the folks running into burning buildings when everyone else is running out—it part of their training and identity as firefighters that they act out every day. As Christians, we similarly act out of our identity as image-bearers of a Holy God.

Duty within Community

The Apostle Paul makes image theology explicit when he writes: "Therefore be imitators of God, as beloved children." (Eph 5:1) Paul draws this theme out in more detail in Galatians 5:16–24, where he contrasts the works of the flesh with the fruits of the spirit, echoing God's self-revelation:

> The LORD passed before him and proclaimed, the LORD, the LORD, a God merciful and gracious, slow to anger, and abounding in steadfast love and faithfulness. (Exod 34:6)

The Apostle Paul also alludes to this verse when he writes about putting off the old self and a putting on the new self in Christ (Eph 4:22–24).

The context for Exodus 34:6 is that God has just given Moses the Ten Commandments for the second time (Exod 20). God disclosed his character as an aid to interpret the Commandments, should anything be unclear. The Commandments themselves served as a thumbnail sketch of each person's duty to God and to the nation of Israel under the Mosaic covenant.

While many people see the Ten Commandments as their duty under the covenant, another way to look at the Commandments is as describing the characteristics of people who identify themselves with the covenantal community. In other words, Christians can be described simply as the people who follow Jesus and obey his commandments (Matt 4:19–20).

Do we act out our duty as members of the Christian

community or simply out of a deeper sense of identity?

Planning and Leadership

Abraham was a man on a mission:

> Now the LORD said to Abram, go from your country and your kindred and your father's house to the land that I will show you. And I will make of you a great nation, and I will bless you and make your name great, so that you will be a blessing. I will bless those who bless you, and him who dishonors you I will curse, and in you all the families of the earth shall be blessed. (Gen 12:1–3)

Abraham became a leader among men, possessing his own private army that conquered the known powers of his day in retrieving his kidnapped nephew, Lot (Gen 14:11–17). But most of his actions were defined by the mission that God gave him: "Go from your country and your kindred and your father's house to the land that I will show you." (Gen 12:1)

God has also given us a mission in the Great Commission: "Go therefore and make disciples of all nations." (Matt 28:19) What is interesting is that when we act out a mission, we also gain an identity.

Vision is important. Knowing that Jesus rose from the dead and will return for us (John 14:3) means that we know the future. It is like having tomorrow's stock report today—we can buy the best stocks without any risk of loss.

Knowing the future is in Christ frees us from worry allowing us to act boldly and take risks to advance God's kingdom today. Like Abraham, we are blessed to be a blessing to others.

Tradeoffs, Desires, and Temptations

> *The fear of the LORD*
> *is the beginning of knowledge;*
> *fools despise wisdom and instruction.*
> (Prov 1:7)

The Bibles teaches ethics through commandments, lists, proverbs, parables, prophecies, colorful stories, and admonitions, which renders any summary of teaching styles incomplete. Many important lessons are subtle.

Be a Good Example

Consider the admonition Jesus offers in the Sermon on the Mount, right after presenting the Beatitudes:

> You are the light of the world. A city set on a hill cannot be hidden. Nor do people light a lamp and put it under a basket, but on a stand, and it gives light to all in the house. In the same way, let your light shine before others, so that they may see your good works and give glory to your Father who is in heaven. (Matt 5:14–16)

This admonition alludes to the creation account in Genesis where it says: "And God said, Let there be light, and there was light." (Gen 1:3) We are to model God's own behavior—providing light—to benefit those around us.

This makes sense because we are created in God's image (Gen 1:27).

Balance is a Virtue

After giving Moses a second set of stone tablets, God instructs Moses on how to interpret the Ten Commandments in view of God's own character—God is merciful, gracious, patient, loving, and faithful (Exod 34:6). If two commandments come in conflict, remember who God is and how he would deal with this conflict—one list (the commandments) is balanced and interpreted by admonitions of a second list (the character traits).

Likewise, when ambiguity arises in our own actions, the same principle applies. Our own character traits aid people in interpreting the righteousness of our actions. Another way to look at these two lists is that the commandments speak to the mind, while the character traits illumines the heart.

Start With the Heart

Jesus' teaching also balances heart and mind. Consider this passage from the Sermon on the Mount:

> You have heard that it was said, you shall not commit adultery. But I say to you that everyone who looks at a woman with lustful

> intent has already committed adultery with her in his heart. (Matt 5:27–28)

Here Jesus places priority on the desires of the heart as the source of sin. In other words, do not consider yourself righteous simply because you have not yet had the opportunity to sin—manage your desires.

Dealing With Temptation

After his baptism but before he began his ministry, the Holy Spirit leads Jesus into the desert where the Devil tempted him, as recorded in the synoptic gospels. Much like Adam and Eve are tempted with food, the Devil goads a hungry Jesus into turning a stone into bread. The Devil tempts Jesus three times. Jesus cites scripture in response to each temptation. In the final temptation, the Devil's temptation starts by misquoting scripture, but Jesus corrects the deception and resists the temptation.

Each temptation Jesus faces is a challenge facing all Christians, particularly leaders. Nouwen (2002, 7–8) summarizes these leadership challenges as the temptation to be relevant (provide food), to be spectacular (show your divinity), and to be powerful (take charge). We want to be relevant, having answers to everyone's questions; we want to be spectacular, showing how God guides our every action and answers our prayers; we want to be powerful, able to lead God's people with clever sermons and drawing large numbers of people to the Gospel.

But rather than yield to these temptations, God asks only that we be fully present in people's lives and faithful in and out of season.

Problem of Boundaries

*B*oundaries define who we are and who we are not. Undefended boundaries are an invitation to abuse and thievery. Whenever pain shows itself, we need to establish a new boundary rule and defend it.

If our primary identity is in Christ, then we emulate Christ in all that we do, our duties in life are defined by Christ, and we act in all things expecting Christ's return. Our boundaries reflect these values in our emotions and thinking.

The Good Samaritan

Cloud and Townsend (1992, 25) explain boundaries in these terms:

> Just as homeowners set out physical property lines around their land, we need to set mental, physical, emotional, and spiritual boundaries for our lives to help us distinguish what is our responsibility and what isn't.

Cloud and Townsend apply their concept of boundaries in interpreting Jesus' parable of the Good Samaritan:

> A man was going down from Jerusalem to Jericho, and he fell among robbers, who stripped him and beat him and departed,

leaving him half dead. Now by chance a priest was going down that road, and when he saw him he passed by on the other side. So likewise a Levite, when he came to the place and saw him, passed by on the other side. But a Samaritan, as he journeyed, came to where he was, and when he saw him, he had compassion. He went to him and bound up his wounds, pouring on oil and wine. Then he set him on his own animal and brought him to an inn and took care of him. And the next day he took out two denarii and gave them to the innkeeper, saying, take care of him, and whatever more you spend, I will repay you when I come back. (Luke 10:30–35)

Why is this called the story of the Good Samaritan rather than the Great Samaritan? The Samaritan did not walk on the other side of the road like the priest or the Levite, which might have been called bad. Neither did he turn the man's situation into a cause, which might have been called great. Instead, the Samaritan focused on what he could do and restored the man to health. Then, he delegated further assistance to the innkeeper and continued his trip (Cloud and Townsend 1992, 38-39).

The Samaritan limited his assistance to that necessary to save the man's life within his own ability to help, thereby demonstrating healthy boundaries. That may sound trivial, but many times I have been paralyzed into inaction thinking that my own efforts at helping people were inadequate. In other words, unable to abolish world hunger, I would flinch at buying a poor beggar lunch. The Samaritan's example suggests that we should not be ashamed at doing what we can—buying lunch—and not worry about changing things that we have no control over.

A Personal Audit

Cloud (2008, 69) suggests that a good place to start working on boundaries in our own lives is to do a life audit, which measures where you spend your time, disconnects between time spent and personal values, and what personal issues contribute to this disconnect. This method of analysis is reminiscent of what Miller and Rollnick (2002, 38) referred to as gap analysis—highlighting the discrepancy between present behavior and broader goals and values.

Christian Boundaries

The concept of boundaries sounds a lot like law, which raises the controversy about the relationship between law and Gospel. In the Gospels, the Pharisees are pictured presenting a narrow interpretation of law to make it doable while Jesus normally widens the interpretation making compliance impossible without divine intervention. Jesus generally speaks about principles while the Pharisees focus on rules.

When the commandments are expressed as principles, sin is also a violation of the principle of love in relationships with God and with neighbor (Matt 22:36–40). Matthew outlines five cases (Matt 5:21, 5:27, 5:33, 5:38, and 5:43) in which Jesus enlarged Mosaic Law by expanding technical compliance to consider underlying attitudes: Murder, adultery, the taking of oaths, and love of neighbor. Jesus introduces each with the expression: "You have heard it said." Consider the case of murder:

> You have heard that it was said to those of old, you shall not murder; and whoever murders will be liable to judgment. But I say to you that everyone who is angry with his brother will be liable to judgment. (Matt 5:21–22).

Jesus sees the act of murder starting with an attitude of anger, which is sinful when it violates the attitude of love and, left unchecked, can lead to murder.

Jesus is not relinquishing the law or diminishing it in any way, as he says: "Do not think that I have come to abolish the Law or the Prophets; I have not come to abolish them but to fulfill them." (Matt 5:17) In this context, fulfilling the law implies a more stringent condition than the law, not a more lenient one, where three states of nature are possible: Noncompliance with law (transgression), technical compliance (Pharisee position), and fulfilling the law (Gospel). Contrasting law and Gospel only compares two of the three states.

By widening the law, Jesus makes it obvious that we must make room in our lives for God and live within his healthy boundaries. The Ten Commandments cannot therefore be abandoned; mere compliance is an indication that we have not centered our lives on Christ. The point is not to try to become the "Great Samaritan," but rather to lean on the Holy Spirit to guide on what to do and what not to do.

Humility and Family Ethics

*H*umility is one of the Christ's defining characteristics. Jesus honors disciples who live humbly, mourn their fallen state, and embody a spirit of meekness. Such disciples will receive heaven and earth (Matt 5:3-5). The Bible illustrates humility in relationships within our families, churches, and communities.

The Christian Family

In Christ, we honor each individual as created in the image of God. The Apostle Paul's writing is particularly clear on this point. He writes: "There is neither Jew nor Greek, there is neither slave nor free, there is no male and female, for you are all one in Christ Jesus." (Gal 3:28) No ethic group is better than any other; no economic class is better than any other; and no gender is better than any other. But Paul goes further in his household codes:

> Children, obey your parents in the Lord, for this is right. Honor your father and mother (this is the first commandment with a promise), that it may go well with you and that you may live long in the land. Fathers, do not provoke your children to anger, but bring them up in the discipline and instruction of the Lord. (Eph 6:1–4)

Because we are all created in the image of God, no age group is better than any other. Neither a newborn nor a senior standing at the gates of heaven is better than one another. Christians are to value life stages equally, honor the current stage, and not cling to any particular stage as if it were intrinsically preferred.

Christianity is a holistic faith that values maturity and embraces each stage of life with equal joy because our faith is rooted in history beginning with creation and ending with Christ's return. Thus, we read:

> I am the Alpha and the Omega, says the Lord God, who is and who was and who is to come, the Almighty. (Rev 1:8)

Knowing the end is in Christ, we can journey through life in Christ meeting the challenges of each stage in life without fear.

Family Function

Consider the challenge of raising children. Research by Stinnett and Beam (1999, 10) reports six characteristics of strong families:

1. Commitment—these families promote each other's welfare and happiness, and value unity.

2. Appreciation and affection—strong families care about each other.

3. Positive and frequent communication.

4. Time together—strong families spend a lot of quality time together.

5. Spiritual well-being—whether or not they attend religious services, strong families have a sense of a greater good or power in life.

6. Ability to cope with stress and crisis—strong families see crises as a growth opportunity.

Here humility is worked out in a family context. A key point in unifying these different models of behavior as it pertains to raising children is that adults are present and fully attentive to the children.

The Family as an Emotional Unit

Family systems theory focuses on "the family as an emotional unit" rather than on particular individuals (Gilbert 2006, 3). This focus runs counter to most counseling approaches that assume the clinical model which treats the individual as autonomous. Problems originating in the family that cause the individual distress cannot be resolved working only with the individual. Family systems theory is often expanded to other emotional units, like offices, churches, and groups, where relationships are intense and span many years.

The emotional unit is sometimes compared to a home plumbing system where, if the water pressure rises to the breaking point, the leak will pop up in the weakest link in the system. For families, the weakest link is usually a child. When parents quarrel continuously, it is often a child that starts acting out (nail biting, bed-wetting, fighting in school, teenage troubles, and so on). If the child sees a therapist alone, the problem is not resolved, because the pressure rises with the parental quarreling, not the child. When the parents stop quarreling, the child often stops acting out (Friedman 1985, 21).

Families matter more than intuition normally suggests. A death in the family may leave one person with chronic migraine headaches; another may develop back pain or experience a heart attack; a third may exhibit psychiatric dysfunction. While this observation may not surprise pastors and chaplains, standard medical and counseling practices assume problems suffered by the individual originate with the individual rather than looking for underlying causes.

Humility as Emotional Maturity

Humility is not shyness and does not arise naturally—it is learned and often comes with emotional maturity. It often brings healing within emotional units because anxiety is infectious (Gilbert 2006, 7).

Gilbert (2006, 7) illustrates this infectious anxiety as like a herd of cattle that are easily spooked and sometimes stampede. Gilbert's grandfather attempts to be a "calming presence" when he is working with the cattle on his farm (Gilbert 2006, 22). When I was a boy, my own grandfather's cattle tolerated my presence when he was present, but became nervous if I stepped into a feedlot alone.

Anxiety transmission is more rapid and intense in tightly "fused" groups where individual are relatively close and unprocessed emotions run wild, so to speak (Gilbert 2006, 21). Anxiety transmission is less rapid and intense in groups with individuals who are "differentiated" where individuals are able to separate feelings from thinking and emotions are less readily shared (Gilbert 2006, 33).

Friedman (1985, 27–31) describes differentiation as the capacity to be an "I" while remaining connected. Differentiation loosens integration, which increases the shock-absorbing capacity of the system. The ideal is to remain engaged in the system in a non-reactive manner—a non-anxious presence. Differentiation may also reduce resistance to change (homeostasis).

Family leaders (including pastors in church families) who increase self-differentiation aid dysfunctional families in healing by reducing stress. Healing takes place through modeling healthy emotions, focusing on problem solving and reducing dysfunctional behaviors—flight, addictions, abuse—that make matters worse.

Ministerial Ethics

*P*astors point people to God. Everything else that they do is a means to that end.

Because God is humbly, but subtly present in our lives, becoming aware of God's Shekinah cloud requires special insight:

> Shekinah is Hebrew word that refers to a collective vision that brings together dispersed fragments of divinity. It is usually understood as a light-disseminating presence bringing an awareness of God to a time and place where God is not expected to be—a place . . . the Shekinah—God's personal presence—and filled that humble, modest, makeshift, sorry excuse for a temple with glory. (Peterson 2011, 100–101)

Without assistance, people are more likely to see Harvey, the six-foot invisible rabbit pictured in the 1950 film by that name, which makes the pastor's role in pointing us to God unique.

The Christian mindset, where Christ is the measure of all things, is unique to Christians. The world sees this mindset as obsession and seldom tolerates it, even among pastors. Blamires (2005, 148) writes:

> For if the Christian faith is true, and the

Christian church the authoritative vehicle of salvation in time, then it is the most urgent, inescapable need of the modern world to adapt itself to the church.

To use a mathematical metaphor, Jesus is my denominator, the measure of all things. With this mindset, the world is ordered and God's Shekinah cloud becomes a reality. Without it, the Shekinah cloud becomes invisible like Harvey, and salvation disappears, becoming illusive, out of reach.

Pastoring by the Numbers

The paying of bills is the bane of pastors.

Taking the Jewish concept of a minion and combining it with the tithe, you get the Old Testament answer to financing a Rabbi. In order to hold a Jewish worship service, a Rabbi needed ten adult men—a minion. If each of these men paid the tithe (which was an obligatory ten percent of income), then the Rabbi would enjoy the same living standard as the average person in his minion.

In a typical American church, people give an average of about one percent of their income. This implies that a pastor's minion is about a hundred families, which is the size of a typical church. The mathematics of church finances suggests why we have seen the growth of mega churches that support a large pastoral staff, numerous programs, and quality music in worship. It also suggests why we have seen preaching increasingly stray from hard teaching and focus on feel-good topics.

Discipling has also suffered. The problem with this arrangement is that pointing someone to God requires intimate knowledge of the person that is acquired only through spending time together. This was entirely possible for a Rabbi with his minion, but seems out of reach for an American pastor with his minion. Intimate communication cannot be one-way communication. Thus, large church concerns about high quality performance and seamless worship services have come at the expense of reduced involvement of the laity in programs, services, and ministries that foster discipleship.

Other Duties as Assigned

The Book of Order 2007/2009 of the Presbyterian Church (USA) describes the duties of a pastor in these terms:

> The permanent pastoral officers of ministers of the Word and Sacrament are pastors and associate pastors. When a minister of the Word and Sacrament is called as a pastor or associate pastor of a particular church

> or churches, she or he is to be responsible for a quality of life and relationships that commend the Gospel to all persons and that communicate its joy and its justice. The pastor is responsible for studying, teaching, and preaching the Word, for administrating Baptism and the Lord's Supper, for praying with and for the congregation. With the elders, the pastor is to encourage the people in the worship and service of God, to equip and enable them for their tasks within the church and their mission in the world; to exercise pastoral care, devoting special attention to the poor, the sick, the troubled, and the dying; to participate in governing responsibilities, including leadership of the congregation in implementing the principles of participation and inclusiveness in the decision making of the church, and its task of reaching out in concern and service to the life of the human community as a whole. With the deacons the pastor is to share in the ministries of sympathy, witness, and service. In addition to these pastoral duties, he or she is responsible for sharing in the ministry of the church in the governing bodies above the session and in ecumenical relationships. (PCUSA 2007, G-6.0202b)

In practice, the only responsibility unique to pastors is the administration of the sacraments. Other responsibilities, including preaching, teaching, leadership, and pastoral care, are shared with others in the church.

Note the bureaucratic nature of this pastoral

definition. First, terms are defined. The office of pastor (and associate pastor) is defined as permanent. Assistant pastors are neither called nor permanent. Second, the call is focused on modeling a quality of life and relationships of the Gospel (not God). Third, responsibilities include studying, teaching, and preaching the Word, administering the sacraments, and praying for the congregation. God himself is not mentioned until the fourth sentence: "The worship and service of God."

The point of discussing other duties as assigned is that the ethics of pastoring requires a clear focus on God that may be hard to maintain within the institution of the church.

Case Studies in Ministry

While ministry is often treated as mysterious, it is a skill that can be learned and improved upon with practice. One way to improve on ministry practice is to work as team and to encourage the team to reflect on and discuss events that do not go as planned using a case study approach.

In their book, *Shared Wisdom: A Guide to Case Study Reflection*, authors Jeffrey Mahan, Barbara Troxell, and

Carol Allen (MTA; 1993, 12–19) see the goal of case studies as to equip a presenter of the case study to return to ministry with greater insight and confidence in themselves and in God's provision and protection.

Case studies assist participants in learning from their mistakes, but focusing on mistakes requires self-awareness and self-disclosure. In a world in which politicians and celebrities daily lose their jobs over a single mistake, even in the church admitting mistakes and focusing on weakness poses a risk. The need for confidentially is accordingly multifaceted—both those studied and those bringing forth the study need to have the process treated confidentially.

MTA (1993, 116–117) recommend a case composed of five parts:

1. Background. Usually a case study focuses on an event described within context.

2. Description. In describing the event, dialogue illustrates what happened and how the presenter responded.

3. Analysis. Identify issues and relationships, with special attention to changes and resistance to change.

4. Evaluation. The presenter assesses their

performance—what worked, what did not work, and why.

5. Theological Reflection. How does our faith inform this event?

The authors suggest that a case study should be about two pages single-spaced and that a presentation should run about an hour.

While the ideal setting for discussion of case studies is with a ministry team, a modified case study can also be useful in writing about ministry. Clearly, the choice of events to study is critical in revealing strengths and weaknesses in ministry. In writing about actual people, however, the case study may need to be recast as a study of a biblical or fictional character so that the privacy of the persons involved is maintained. In preaching, this often ends up being an "I know a person who" story from the pastor giving the talk (Savage 1996, 89–92).

Presuppositional Ethics

*M*uch of ethical training is unconsciously absorbed from our surroundings in the home, church, and society. Even formal ethics training in our offices typically focuses on the minimum legal requirement for the office to escape legal liability under specific rules, regulations, or laws. The real business of ethical behavior is seldom discussed, taught, or even codified. Even the Christian faith itself is more caught than taught, meaning that it is learned more by osmosis than by formal training. In philosophy, this implicit knowledge is referred to as a presupposition.

Most of the time in theology, philosophy, and ethics, we assume a cognitive approach to learning. The presumption is that human beings are essentially rational and that faith itself is a rational undertaking. The classical focus on virtue, character development, and establishing good habits seldom receives much attention. The Bible suggests that this cognitive approach has two important limitations in discussing ethics and faith.

Creation Influences Thought

The first limitation arises because we are created, male and female, in the image of a triune God. Being created to live and reproduce in families implies that we experience the world in community. Much as we want our independence, our thoughts, feelings, and language are not entirely our own.

Being created in the image of a triune God reinforces a focus on community. The Bible portrays God as Father, Son, and Holy Spirit—a complete community in the godhead, as Jesus references after the Last Super:

> But when the Helper comes, whom I will send to you from the Father, the Spirit of truth, who proceeds from the Father, he will bear witness about me. (John 15:26)

In imaging a triune God—Father, Son, and Holy Spirit—we image a community, something we can neither fully embody nor understand. By contrast, a unitary god is fixed, stable, and offers mostly an opportunity for self-projection, where a triune God is dynamic, engaging, and alive.

In particular, the language we speak shapes our perceptions of reality in fundamental ways, not the least of which is that it reflects the culture we live and worship in. Our attitudes about gender, work, faith, and many other things are embedded in the words that we use and do not use. We are not alone in this world. We carry our community with us wherever we go.

The Hebrew Heart

The second limitation of the cognitive approach arises out of who we are. In the Hebrew mindset assumed in the New Testament, mind and body differ as parts within a unified whole, whose center is the heart, while the Greeks distinguished mind and body as separate. Confusion arises when we assume incorrectly that the New Testament sees the heart as a body part and we treat heart and mind as separated, like the Greeks and most secular people.

This confusion implies that the cognitive approach cannot fully inform our faith because it is based on faulty Greek anthropology. As theologian James K.A. Smith (2016, 2) writes:

> Jesus is a teacher who doesn't inform our intellect but forms our very loves. . . . His teaching doesn't just touch the calm, cool, collected space of reflection and contemplation, he is a teacher who invades

> the heated, passionate regions of the heart. He is the Word who penetrates even dividing the soul and spirit; he judges the thoughts and attitudes of the heart. (Heb 4:12)

Inherent in this statement is the Hebrew view of anthropology cited above—note the two references to heart. What Greek would talk about "the thoughts and attitudes of the heart"?

Drawing attention to this anthropology, Smith (2016, 5) asks: "Do you ever experience a gap between what you know and what you do?" If Smith had the rational mind in view, no such gap would exist, but we all experience this gap.

This line of thought leads Smith (2016, 7) to observe: "What if you are defined not by what you know [the mind] but by what you desire? [the heart]" If our desires are reflected more in our actions than in our words, then this Hebrew anthropology leads us immediately into an inconvenient discussion of ethics because our hearts are not as lily-white clean as our words. It also forces us to discuss how we know what we know (the epistemology question) because our hearts are not so easily persuaded to follow our own thoughts. Suddenly, much of the New Testament language sounds less churchy and more informed by an alternative worldview, one decidedly not Greek.

Clearly, we cannot talk about thinking independent of feelings or independent of the communities in which we reside and worship. We need to treat them as interdependent. Still, we need to understand better how we know what we know before we can even talk about our faith.

Ethical Teaching in the Psalms

An important example of ethics being taught through osmosis is found in the liturgical use of the psalms. Wenham (2012, 1–2) writes:

> It is the ethic taught by the liturgy of the Old Testament, the Psalter, that is the focus of this book. The psalms were sung in the first and second temples, and in the subsequent two millennia they have been reused in the prayers of the Jewish synagogue and the Christian church. As we will see, the psalms have much to say about behavior, about what actions please God and what he hates, so that anyone praying them is simultaneously being taught an ethic.

Wenham (2012, 7) goes on to explain:

> This book, then, is an attempt to begin to deal with a blind spot in current biblical and theological thinking. I have called it

> Psalms as Torah out of my conviction that the psalms were and are vehicles not only of worship but also of instruction, which is the fundamental meaning of Torah, otherwise rendered "law." From the very first psalm, the Psalter presents itself as a second Torah, divided into five books like the Pentateuch, and it invited its readers to meditate on them day and night, just as Joshua was told to meditate on the law of Moses. (Ps 1.2; Josh 1:8)

A key insight that Wenham offers is the effect of memorization and putting the Psalms to music on ethical teaching.

Wenham notes that many Psalms are written in the first person. Repeating such psalms in prayer or song accordingly is like repeating a vow before God, yourself, and others. He writes:

> If we praise a certain type of behavior in our prayers, we are telling God that this is how we intend to behave. On the other hand, if in prayer we denounce certain acts and pray for God to punish them, we are in effect inviting God to judge us if we do the same. This makes the ethics of liturgy uniquely powerful. It makes a stronger claim on the believer than either law, wisdom, or story, which are simply subject to passive reception: one can listen to a proverb or a story and then take it or leave it, but if you pray ethically, you commit yourself to a path of action. (Wenham 2012, 57)

Because many of us grew up singing hymns and liturgy inspired by Psalms, this tradition helped insulate us from less reflective and negative influences that seem so pervasive today.

Risk Takers for Christ

*J*esus teaches us to watch for his return. Mark 13:33 reads: "Take heed, keep on the alert; for you do not know when the appointed time will come." Likewise, Luke 12:35 echoes the Parable of the Ten Virgins: "Be dressed in readiness, and keep your lamps lit." Directly after the Parable of the Ten Virgins in Matthew 25 we read the Parable of the Talents that not only advises watchfulness, but guides us on how to wait.

The Parable of the Talents starts with advice about being watchful, but then goes on:

> For it will be like a man going on a journey, who called his servants and entrusted to them his property. To one he gave five talents, to another two, to another one, to each according to his ability. Then he went away. (Matt 25:14–15)

We are then told how the first two servants invest the master's money and double his principal, while the third servant buries the master's money in ground.

When the master returns, he settles accounts with each of the servants. The first two servants present the master with his principal and the earnings from their investments. In both cases, the master responds with the same statement: "Well done, good and faithful servant. You have been faithful over a little; I will set you over much. Enter into the joy of your master." (Matt 25:21,23)

In contrast to the first two servants' risk-taking, the third servant acts out of fear:

> Master, I knew you to be a hard man, reaping where you did not sow, and gathering where you scattered no seed, so I was afraid, and I went and hid your talent in the ground. Here, you have what is yours. (Matt 25:24–25)

The master calls this servant "wicked and slothful" and parrots the servant's suggestion that he is a hard man, suggesting agreement, but he goes on to suggest: "Then you ought to have invested my money with the bankers, and at my coming I should have received what was my own with interest." (Matt 25:27) In so many words, the master suggests that the third servant is both cowardly and imprudent, because depositing the money with a banker requires accepting very little risk of financial loss. The master takes the money given to the third servant and gives it to the first. Then, the third servant is described as worthless and condemned to perdition, a penalty too harsh for most postmodern people to even to hear.

So what do we learn from this parable?

The first thing to note is the context. Immediately after the Parable of the Talents is another parable of judgment, where the goats and the sheep are separated. Then, in chapter 26 of Matthew, we read:

> When Jesus had finished all these sayings, he said to his disciples, You know that after two days the Passover is coming, and the Son of Man will be delivered up to be crucified. (Matt 26:1–2)

The implication is that the three parables in chapter 25 are given to prepare the disciples for Jesus' death, resurrection, and second coming. All three suggest that the disciples should be watchful of Christ's return, but only the Parable of the Talents suggests how to spend the time while Jesus is absent.

The lesson here is that knowing that Christ will return, we should be cheerful, not fearful, in our work as we take risks to advance the Kingdom of God. Cheerful risk takers, not fearful hoarders, are the good and faithful servants.

CHARACTER

As Christians, our character should conform to the image of Christ under the mentorship of the Holy Spirit. Conformation requires learning, interpreting, and adjusting to Christ's image. Context matters; effort is required. We are formed by our good habits and malformed by the bad. If we succeed, we are blessed to be a blessing.

Ethical Perspective

Christian ethics is not a branch of philosophy, but is how we live out our relationship to God.

Jesus gives an analogy:

> I am the true vine, and my Father is the vinedresser. Every branch in me that does not bear fruit he takes away, and every branch that does bear fruit he prunes, that it may bear more fruit. Already you are clean because of the word that I have spoken to you. Abide in me, and I in you. As the branch cannot bear fruit by itself, unless it abides in the vine, neither can you, unless you abide in me. I am the vine; you are the branches. Whoever abides in me and I in him, he it is that bears much fruit, for apart from me you can do nothing. (John 15:1–5)

For me, this analogy evokes the picture of an electric appliance that is useless until it is plugged in—the power is in the cord, not the appliance (Bridges 1996, 61). Christians rely, not on a philosophical approach to determine our actions, but on the inspiration of the Holy Spirit.

Robinson (2004, 124) illustrates this principle when she writes:

> When you encounter another person, when have dealings with anyone at all, it is as if

a question is being put to you. So you must think, What is the Lord asking of me in this moment, in this situation?

The guidance of the Holy Spirit is critical in Christian decisions because they cannot be divorced from their context.

Ethical Dimensions

Suppose a man is shot dead. From an ethical perspective, we must immediately ask: What is the relationship between the shooter and the dead man? Was the shooting intentional or accidental, and how do we know? What led up to the shooting? What was the shooter's emotional state of mind? Where the dead man and the shooter from the same ethnic group? What were their roles in this shooting? From a legal perspective, a public inquiry may be required to sort all these questions out before a court decides what to do about the shooting.

The shooting of an unarmed man in his own home in Dallas, Texas, in 2019 is a case in point. An off-duty, white officer, tired from a long shift walked into the wrong apartment thinking it was her own and mistakenly shot and killed the apartment owner, a black man.

At least three people are involved in this example:

Character 81

The dead man, the shooter, and a judge. Each will have a perspective on this shooting and the community may be divided on how to interpret this shooting. Ethics always involves interpretation. This implies that the philosophical precedents guiding the shooter could be different from the perspectives of every other participant in this event. The emotional mindset of each participant has a bearing on the interpretation rendered, but the precedents guiding the shooter do not automatically exonerate the actions taken.

With the entire world watching, the jury found the officer guilty of murder, a highly unusual outcome to a unique set of circumstances (Thebault and Shammas 2019).

The Christian guided by the Holy Spirit has an advantage in dealing ethically with a situation because God alone knows all the relevant factors to consider and the eventual outcome. Mere ethical knowledge pales in comparison as a guide to behavior because we never control all the factors influencing the ethical interpretation of an event by all the participants.

Interpreting Life

The defining characteristic of the postmodern era is uncertainty. Uncertainty compounded by a lack of consensus on basic values and the rapid pace of changes in technology and social conventions that challenge ethical behavior.

Postmodern uncertainty is also in sharp contrast with the stability of traditional society where tradition informs every important decision in one's life—what gender roles we follow, who our friends are, who we marry, what profession we take up, and who and how we worship. Life has meaning in a traditional society because this guidance was accepted and rewarded with status and honor.

Postmodern culture questions tradition and focuses on the individual who is responsible for every imaginable decision with little or no guidance. If we succeed as postmodern individuals, we are fully employed, have a medical plan, and can buy stuff, but we have no guarantee of status and honor because the culture's standards keep morphing. Thus, anxiety has become a defining characteristic of our time.

The Indeterminacy Problem

Postmodern anxiety and uncertainty point to a more general problem of indeterminacy that is typically masked when we act on consensus or do not reflect on our experiences.

Indeterminacy arise in statistics because we know that correlation does not indicate causality. In theory, many causes can explain a particular correlation, so a theory is required to suggest the cause of an observed correlation. Otherwise, the relationship could be entirely random. If sunspots are associated with weather on earth, what explains this relationship? (Greene 1997, 816) Superstition can be defined as resulting from a random association being confused with a causal relationship—if having a black cat cross your path is a bad omen, exactly how does this omen translate into outcomes?

The Rorschach (inkblot) test provides an interesting application of this indeterminacy problem (Smith 2001, 205–206). When a psychiatrist shows a patient a random inkblot and the patients sees patterns in the inkblot, the patterns arise from the patient's preconceptions being imposed on the inkblot. Does the patient see angels or demons? Beautiful women or monsters? These preconceptions (or random associations) provide insight into the interior life of the patient because the patterns projected on the inkblot belong entirely to the patient.

Telling a Faithful Story

The anxiety and uncertainty of postmodern society poses the Christian leader with a kind of cultural inkblot test. How can leadership successfully navigate through this perilous test?

One answer can be taken from my earlier comments on the book, *Crucial Conversations*, where I noted four stages in a dialogue: Presenting facts (see and hear), telling a story, feeling, and acting (PGMS 2012, 110). The authors observed that once emotions take over, actions get locked in. The formation of productive stories presents the last best chance to channel a dialog towards useful action.

An infinite number of stories can be told, but not all comport well with the facts or are organizationally helpful. Three kinds of unproductive (clever) stories—victim, villain, and helpless stories—arise that are usually counter-productive (PGMS 2012, 116–119). Claiming victimhood means accepting no responsibility for what happens next. Pointing a finger at a villain or claiming a lack of power to change things is likewise an attempt to absolve oneself from any responsibility.

In the context of a faith community, it is more productive to tune into the church's history and to compare it with other faithful churches or stories from the Bible.

The Example of Barnabas

The history of many faithful churches parallels the story of Barnabas. In his book, *Becoming Barnabas: The Ministry of Encouragement,* Paul Moots (2014, 2–3) writes:

> The ministry of encouragement is the art of leading and supporting others in the discovery of their own spiritual gifts and call to discipleship ... We can become a Barnabas ... Encouragement allows the congregation to shape its ministry around its strengths rather than to base its work on some model derived from another congregation's story, another pastor's experience.

Notice the role of story in this description. Each of us and each congregation has its own story of its Christian walk that deserves to be honored and built on.

In Hebrew, Barnabas literally means *son of the prophet*, but Luke gives it a metaphorical translation: *Son of encouragement*. Interestingly, it is also a nickname given to Joseph, a Levite from Cyprus (Acts 4:36).

Encouragement is at the heart of the multiplication of gifts and church growth (Moots 2014, 6). It stands in contrast to the usual concept of discipling that implicitly (or explicitly) defines discipling almost exclusively in a teacher-student role and seeks more to replicate than to strengthen. At the heart of encouragement is respect, much like Barnabas respected Paul.

Learning to Tack

One pleasure that I had as a camp counselor in high school was learning to sail. Sailboats differ from other boats in being powered by wind rather than someone rowing or by an engine. Winds change. Sailors need to prepare themselves for every eventually. Television ads always picture sailboats speeding along with a good tailwind, but experienced sailors know that tailwinds are an exception, not the rule.

When the wind changes, the rudder and sails must adjust to make maximum use of the wind's force. The hardest maneuver is to sail into the wind because the boat must zigzag back and forth into the wind—tack—with little, if any, efficiency in moving forward. The only thing worse than headwinds are the doldrums, when the wind simply disappears.

Postmodern Sailing

Being stuck between the headwinds and the doldrums aptly describes postmodern life. The American dream of a college education followed by a good paying job, which your parents and grandparent enjoyed, now seems illusive and out of reach for many young people. Years of hard labor in school are more likely followed by a minimum wage job and crushing student debt.

Headwinds and the doldrums are not just a problem for the young. Even well-educated and experienced seniors must frequently reinvent their careers late in life as companies restructure and offer little prospect for a pension or a health plan for most employees laid off. Suicide rates in the United States are at record high levels, with suicide among older men showing the largest increases. For years, bankruptcy rates in the United States were closely tied to a family medical emergency—what do you do if you lose your job and your health plan is tied to your employment?

Storm on the Galilee

The New Testament contains several sailing analogies, as we read:

> And leaving the crowd, they took him with them in the boat, just as he was. And other boats were with him. And a great windstorm arose, and the waves were breaking into the boat, so that the boat was already filling. But he was in the stern, asleep on the cushion. And they woke him and said to him, Teacher, do you not care that we are perishing? And

> he awoke and rebuked the wind and said to the sea, Peace! Be still! And the wind ceased, and there was a great calm. (Mark 4:36–39)

What is most striking about this story is that many of Jesus' disciples were professional fishermen and expert sailors. When an expert comes to you for advice in their area of expertise, you know that you are in serious trouble. Yet, instinctively the disciples turn to Jesus with well-founded fears, and Jesus calms the wind and the sea.

Two points come to mind in reading this account of the near-drowning experience of the disciples and Jesus.

The first point is that this story occurs early in Jesus' ministry and the storm on the Galilee is a kind of communal baptism for the disciples. Ministry is not a walk in the park. Early in my seminary journey I hung a copy of Rembrandt's painting, the Storm on the Galilee, in my kitchen and it became the inspiration for the cover of my book, *Simple Faith*.

The second point is reinforced by the context in Mark—the next story is the healing of the demoniac, a kind of resurrection story. Immersion baptism is a symbolic death and resurrection; sprinkling baptism is more of a symbolic cleansing. The near drowning of the disciples in the Sea of Galilee is more of an immersion experience!

Jesus' admonition to the disciples remains valid today: "Why are you so afraid? Have you still no faith?" (Mark 4:40) When the headwinds blow, the water rises, and our expertise fails, we need to turn to Jesus in faith rather than in fear.

Anger and Murder

> *You shall not murder.* (Exod 20:13)

The Sixth Commandment—you shall not murder—seems cut and dry. The Bible repeats it five times using the exact same words (Deut 5:17, Exod 20:13, Matt 5:21, Matt 19:18, Rom 13:9). The punishment for murder—death—is given in the account of Noah (Gen 9:11).

Jesus compares murder with being angry with your brother or sister. He then comments:

> [If] your brother has something against you, leave your gift there before the altar and go. First be reconciled to your brother, and then come and offer your gift. (Matt 5:24)

This comment is interesting for two reasons. First, at the time when he spoke, only priests were allowed to enter the Holy Place in the Temple and approach the altar. Second, this comment appears to make reconciliation with our brother or sister more important than reconciliation with God.

What is that about? Jesus is reminding his listeners not of the Temple, but of the first murder story in the Bible—the story of Cain and Abel. Cain got angry with his brother,

Abel, after Abel brought a more acceptable sacrifice to God. For this, Cain murdered Abel (Gen 4:1–8). Jesus' point is that we should reconcile with each other before anger gets out of control and before we do something that we may later regret (Matt 5:23–24).

Jesus makes two important points.

First, Jesus teaches us to prevent murder by removing the incentive to murder. This lesson can then be applied to all sorts of situations, not just murder.

Second, asking God for forgiveness (bringing a gift) does not erase the sin that we have committed against one another. If we murder someone, asking God's forgiveness does not restore the life lost or heal the emotional devastation experienced by the victim's family. Forgiveness cannot be just about words.

Asking God for forgiveness, such as repeating a prayer of confession on Sunday morning, neither requires a change of attitude towards our sin (Jesus' first point) nor compensating those hurt by what we have done (Jesus' second point). True repentance (a real change in heart) answers the first point; making restitution (compensating our victims) answers the second point.

Does Jesus' lesson mean that we should never be angry? No. Anger has an object. Some objects of our anger are selfish and evil; some are not. Jesus got angry about injustice at least twice: About those doing business in the temple (John 2:14–17) and about the hard-hearted Pharisees who refused to allow good works, such as healing, on the Sabbath (Mark 3:5).

Jesus admonishes us to check our anger to avoid even bigger problems.

Spiritual Disciplines

If Jesus is the vine and we are the branches, then staying attached to the vine is our first priority. The First Commandment makes this point: "You shall have no other gods before me." (Exod 20:3) John's Gospel goes a step further declaring Jesus as the ethical image of God with God during creation:

> He was in the beginning with God. All things were made through him, and without him was not anything made that was made. In him was life, and the life was the light of men. The light shines in the darkness, and the darkness has not overcome it. (John 1:2–5)

In describing Jesus as the light of the world, John draws our attention to God's first refinement—creating light—after creating heaven and earth (Gen 1:3). The implication is that creation itself started with an ethical intent, which we share in by virtue of being created in God's own image (Gen 1:27).

Two Objectives of Spiritual Disciplines

In his Sermon on the Mount, Jesus uses this same light metaphor of his disciples:

> You are the light of the world. A city set on a hill cannot be hidden. Nor do people light a lamp and put it under a basket, but on a stand, and it gives light to all in the house. In the same way, let your light shine before others, so that they may see your good works and give glory to your Father who is in heaven. (Matt 5:14–16)

The implication here is that staying attached to the vine is the first priority and that the purpose of this attachment is to convey light, an ethical mandate. Thus, for Christians, spiritual disciplines serve to increase our openness to God's blessings and extend them to others (Gen 12:1–3; Matt 22:36–40).

Rapprochement

The eating of forbidden fruit led to humanity's expulsion from the Garden of Eden. Banishment is a penalty reserved for rebels and it creates a physical barrier between us and God that only God can overcome. For as creator of the universe, God stands outside of time and space while we remain within time and space, unable to bridge the gap on our own.

Implicit in taking Christ as our model is that Jesus is the divine image in which we were created. As both God and human, Jesus Christ, our great High Priest, is able to bridge the gap that we cannot (e.g. Heb 9:11–13).

In dying on the cross, Christ paid the penalty for our sin, but our remoteness from God requires rapprochement. We must accept Christ's sacrifice on our behalf and be willing to admit God into our lives. Admitting God into our lives—our sanctification—has three parts: Renouncing sin (practicing holiness), taking on the attributes of Christ (pursuing godliness), and reconciling with those who we have sinned against (social ministry).

How we approach practicing holiness and pursuing godliness naturally depends on the sins that we are most prone to commit. A glutton is likely to benefit most from fasting while a workaholic should consider practicing Sabbath rest. In a fractured world where people hide themselves from the consequences of their collective actions, social ministry might be seen as a particularly important sanctification activity.

Dancing With God

Sanctification is like taking God as a dancing partner. Accepting an invitation to dance is a verbal commitment, but dancing requires coordinated movement between two people. One would never claim the title of dancer having only accepted an invitation to dance. Neither would anyone enter a dance competition without practice. Faith is like accepting a lifelong challenge to become the best dancer one can be.

The Value of Life

The Lord's Prayer reminds us to honor God's name in keeping with the Third Commandment—do not take the Lord's name in vain—because all the other commandments are leveraged on it (Exod 20:7). Why keep the other commandments, if we dishonor God's name? Dishonoring God devalues human life because we are created in God' image.

Intrinsic Versus Market Value

The practical implications of honoring God arise because we are created in God's image, which gives human life intrinsic value—value in itself that does not change with life's circumstances. Because life has intrinsic value, we cannot accept discrimination, injustice, abuse, mistreatment of prisoners, weapons of mass destruction, euthanasia, abortion, designer babies, and a host of other detestable practices. Human rights—a concept based on intrinsic value—exist because we are created in the image of a Holy God.

Our capitalist society focuses, not on intrinsic values, but on market values. Market values change with volatile circumstances. Your market value as a person implicitly depends on your productivity. If you are young, old, or unable to work, then you are a dependent and a burden on working people. The focus on market values inherently disrespects God's image. When God is not honored, neither are we.

The strong influence of market values on our self-image explains, in part, why depression rates tend to be highest among population groups who are unable to work. The rate of depression, suicide, anxiety disorders, addictions, and divorce appear to be correlated with changing job prospects.

Honor and Idolatry

When God's name is dishonored, we also become more prone to idolatry (Rom 1:21–23). Why worship the God of the Bible when my income and status in society depends more on my family legacy, education, and hard work? So I naturally run to substitutes for God that work, like insurance, to manage the ups and downs of life. Alternatively, I can obsess about the security of my home, spouse, and family.

The implications of honoring the name of God come together in the debate over euthanasia—the right to die. If my self-image and my dignity in society are both increasingly subjected to the same market values, then I will surrender myself to assisted suicide precisely when I need support from my family. And, of course, they will agree because I have become a burden both financially and emotionally. Consequently, euthanasia is evil masquerading as compassion. We are created in the image of a holy God who declares that life is good and sacred (Gen 1:31).

Link to Ethics

Ethics focuses on living out your faith.

When someone is speaking, do you honor them by listening or go to that happy place in your mind? Do you know the name of the janitor in your office or only the names of your supervisors? How do you show that the people in your life, including those really annoying people, are created in the image of God?

Ethics is about who we honor and the choices we make.

Ninevites

No two doctrines of the church are further from the hearts of Americans than the doctrines of election and judgment. Richard Niebuhr (1937, 137) characterized liberal Protestant theology:

> A God without wrath brought men without sin into a kingdom without judgment through the ministration of a Christ without a cross.

Without judgment there can be no election because the two doctrines are mirror images of one another. Still, election is misunderstood as a kind of holy huddle, when it is at the heart of salvation and the antithesis to judgment.

Blessed to be a Blessing

In her book, *Re-Imaging Election*, Suzanne McDonald (2010, 190–191) observes that the holy huddle is a modern myth writing: "Election is the expression of—and the chosen means to further—the triune God's purpose of blessing." The interpretative verse arises in the covenant of God with Abraham:

> Now the LORD said to Abram, go from your country and your kindred and your father's house to the land that I will show you. And

> I will make of you a great nation, and I will bless you and make your name great, so that you will be a blessing. I will bless those who bless you, and him who dishonors you I will curse, and in you all the families of the earth shall be blessed. (Gen 12:1–3)

This covenant begins with a stipulation: "Go from your country and your kindred and your father's house." In modern parlance, Abraham, grow up and stand on your own feet. If Abraham is willing to take the risk of becoming an independent adult by leaving his father's protection, connections, and wealth, then God says he will bless him to become a blessing to others. Even before the establishment of the nation of Israel, God has laid out his plan to evangelize the world, anticipating the Great Commission (Matt 28:19–20).

The parable of the Prodigal Son (Luke 15:11–15) depicts the younger son that "took a journey into a far country" as the son who eventually comes to love and appreciate his father. Thus, the inward-looking church—the holy huddle—appears more like the spiteful, older son who stayed home and, in terms of the covenant, refused to be a blessing to others.

Sodom and Gomorrah

The story of the destruction of Sodom and

Gomorrah is often interpreted primarily in terms of the judgment of God on these two cities for their sexual sin, including homosexual sin. Yet, the context of the story is a dialogue between God and Abraham that begins with:

> The LORD said, Shall I hide from Abraham what I am about to do, seeing that Abraham shall surely become a great and mighty nation, and all the nations of the earth shall be blessed in him? (Gen 18:17–18)

While the judgment of the cities is topical, the story focuses on Abraham's handling of God's disclosure. What does Abraham do? Abraham immediately intercedes for Sodom and Gomorrah, knowing that his self-absorbed nephew, Lot, lives near Sodom.

The key phrase in Abraham's intercession is: "Will you [God] indeed sweep away the righteous with the wicked?" (Gen 18:23) God does not spare the cities, but he does send his angel to rescue Lot and his family.

In this passage, God reveals his judgment to Abraham, a stand in for the rest of us, to see how Abraham will react. In this example, Abraham passes the test when he exhibits compassion for the cities and engages God in intercessory prayer.

The Reluctant Prophet

How many of us would pass God's test of Abraham? In scripture, the counter-example to Abraham arises in the story of the Prophet Jonah. In this short story, we read:

> Now the word of the LORD came to Jonah the son of Amittai, saying, Arise, go to Nineveh, that great city, and call out against it, for their evil has come up before me. (Jonah 1:1–2)

God's disclosure to Jonah is similar to that of Abraham. Nineveh is another evil city that God told his prophet that he would destroy. But unlike Sodom and Gomorrah, God offers the city an alternative by sending Jonah to "call out against it."

Nineveh was the hometown of Sennacherib king of Assyria, who had seized all of Judea, except for Jerusalem (Isa 36:1). Jonah hated the Ninevites and, instead of going to preach God's mercy to them, he got on a ship to escape from God and his mission. Then, as every Sunday school kid knows, a storm came up, the sailors tossed Jonah overboard, and he is swallowed by a whale that, after three days, spits him up on a beach. God then repeats his request for Jonah to go to Nineveh. Listen to why Jonah refused to go:

> And he prayed to the LORD and said, O LORD, is not this what I said when I was yet in my country? That is why I made haste to flee to Tarshish; for I knew that you are a gracious God and merciful, slow to anger and abounding in steadfast love, and relenting from disaster. (Jonah 4:2)

In this response, Jonah recites Exodus 34:6, which recounts God's character traits. Knowing God is merciful, Jonah refused to preach repentance to the Ninevites, but later does so reluctantly and they do repent, averting God's wrath, much to Jonah's consternation (Jonah 3:10, 4:1).

Judgment and End Times

Knowing that we are blessed to be a blessing and that God shares his plans for judgment with us through scripture and revelation, our attitude about those under judgment should change. Judgment of those outside the community of faith comes as a test of the hearts for those inside the community. Think about John's prophecy about the end times:

> The nations raged, but your wrath came, and the time for the dead to be judged, and for rewarding your servants, the prophets and saints, and those who fear your name, both small and great, and for destroying the destroyers of the earth. (Rev 11:18)

Do we cheer the destruction of sinners, like Jonah, or

intercede in prayer, like Abraham? Scripture clearly shows that God's heart runs to mercy quicker than ours.

Creation Living

How does creation fit into your spirituality?

Myself, when I am anxious at the end of the day, I retire with a good book to my front porch to enjoy a cool breeze, listen to the birds, and watch the sun set through the trees. Here God's presence comforts me.

Spiritual Roots to Ecological Sensitivity

One of my earliest and most enduring influences was Henry David Thoreau's *Walden*. He begins:

> When I wrote the following pages, or rather the bulk of them, I lived alone, in the woods, a mile from any neighbor, in a house which I built myself, on the shore of Walden Pond, in Concord, Massachusetts, and earned my living by the labor of my hands only. I lived there two years and two months. At present I am a sojourner to civilized life again. (Thoreau 1960, 1)

He goes on to explain:

> I wanted to live deep and suck out all the marrow of life, to live so sturdily and Spartan-like as to put to rout all that was not life, to cut a broad swath and shave close, to drive life into a corner, and reduce to its lowest terms. (Thoreau 1960, 62–63)

The idea of a Spartan existence, which he immediately related to reformed spirituality by paraphrasing the Westminster Shorter Catechism, always had a special appeal to me:

> Q: What is the chief end of man?
>
> A: Man's chief end is to glorify God, and to enjoy him forever. (PCUSA 1999, 7.001)

Exposed to the Genesis account of the Garden of Eden and to Thoreau, I have always associated creation with spirituality. My first career as an agricultural economist manifested this belief (MMRB 1975). However, it took a recent reading of *Thirsty for God* by Bradley Holt (2017, 31) to remind me of my own spiritual roots in this regard.

Genesis describes the earth as God's creation (Gen 1:1) over which the Holy Spirit hovers (Gen 1:2). We are created in God's image (Gen 1:27) and given the mandate to be fruitful and multiply (Gen 1:28). Later, God created the Garden of Eden (Gen 2:8) and put man into it to "keep it" (Gen 2:15). Reluctant gardeners, perhaps, Adam and Eve sin (Gen 3:6) and are driven out of the garden (Gen 3:24). Original sin not only separated us from communion with God, it introduced tension into our relationship with creation and our intended stewardship role.

The Apostle Paul speaks of this tension, writing:

> For we know that the whole creation has been groaning together in the pains of childbirth until now. And not only the creation, but we ourselves, who have the first fruits of the Spirit, groan inwardly as we wait eagerly for adoption as sons, the redemption of our bodies. (Rom 8:22–23)

In the hours immediately before his arrest, Jesus retired to the Garden at Gethsemane to pray. Some have interpreted this retreat to Gethsemane as a kind of return to Eden.

This return to Eden motif is not the only connection between Jesus and the creation accounts. When asked about divorce in Matthew 19:3–9, Jesus cites Genesis 1:27, which references God's divine image, from the creation accounts and explicitly criticizes Moses' later teaching on divorce (Deut 24:1–3) as a consequence of a hardened heart. Later, when criticized for his disciple's singing on entering Jerusalem, Jesus puts the Pharisees in their place, citing: "Out of the mouth of babies and infants, you have established strength" (Ps 8:2a) and inferring (a subtle slam) the second half of the sentence: "Because of your foes, to still the enemy and the avenger." (Ps 8:2b) Psalm 8 is also a creation psalm that Jesus (and his audience) had obviously committed to memory (Spangler and Tverberg 2009, 37).

Ecological Anxiety

In recent years, anxiety about the fragility of our earth's environment has reached a fever pitch. Where nineteenth century anxiety focused on limits to the quantity of food available to feed a growing population, recent concerns about global warming might be described as prophecy of an ecological Armageddon. How should Christians respond to these concerns?

Few scientists question that the earth is warming. The opening of Northwest Passage from the Atlantic to Pacific oceans that had been icebound in the nineteenth century, reminds us that global warming is taking place. Less certain is the question of what can be done about it?

What is Our Mandate?

Because the science and politics of global warming are not easily discerned, I do not profess to have an answer or the ability to direct a solution. My personal limitations, however, do not relinquish me of responsibly as a steward of creation. As Christians, we should refuse to play the victim or the villain, or to claim that we are powerless in any endeavor. Neither should we abdicate our responsibility to politicians eager to shut down debate and rush to imprudent solutions (Goldberg 2009, 382).

We can do a number of things:

1. We can pray for the Holy Spirit to sustain us and our planet.

2. We can inform ourselves and others about ecological matters.

3. We can reduce our consumption of energy and products known to create environmental hazards.

Following Thoreau, we can live a Spartan lifestyle as a spiritual discipline, mindful of God's provision and thankful for his protection.

Waste not; want not.

Sunshine and Exercise

> *We rejoice in our sufferings, knowing that suffering produces endurance, and endurance produces character, and character produces hope.*
> (Rom 5:3–4)

In April 2019 as I finished publishing my book, *Simple Faith*, I burned myself out. Physically and emotionally exhausted, my motivation also flatlined. I thought that if I take it easy a couple weeks, I would bounce back. Weeks passed with no bounce back. In writing and editing I had clearly pushed myself too far this time.

Burnout's Physical Component

During my eight months of editing that year, I had often cheated on my daily routine reducing the distance in swimming to only a quarter mile. This presumably allowed me more time to work, but it also allowed my stress levels to build up and contributed to a problem of weight gain. Being busy, I felt too distracted to enjoy my daily swim.

By June, I had returned to my usual routine of swimming half a mile a day, but returning to my old routine did nothing to relieve the burnout. However, I noticed that my burnout was more pronounced in the evening, much like sunset dementia—a condition where Alzheimer's patients manifest dementia more obviously when tired at the end of the day.

At first this observation really bothered me—am I beginning to manifest Alzheimer's disease, like my father or my grandmother? In prayer, I found the strength to take another interpretation. If burnout had a physical component, then a physical solution was warranted.

Negative Self-Talk

Initially, this insight helped little. I said to myself, what good is this? I barely have the energy to complete my workout, let alone step it up. One day, joking with a friend in the gym, I even made fun of myself: "What am I going to do, buy a pair of running shoes and start running intervals?" Then I thought, why not? I haven't had a knee problem since the 1990s. Perhaps, I could cross train and avoid knee injuries this time.

Physical Training

In July, I ordered a pair of running shoes online. In the days after placing the order, I was so uncertain about my ability to jog again that, when they arrived, I hid them from my wife, thinking she would ridicule me for wasting my money on such a foolish idea. Still, I put on a new set of shorts and new tee-shirt, and started jogging every other day, hoping that no one would see me.

To keep things easy, I began running intervals. Jog a hundred paces, then walk a hundred paces. Days became weeks. Three months into jogging, I abandoned running intervals to jog continuously at a slow pace.

By the end of September, I never felt better. Although my workout leaves me physically exhausted, the burnout has gone; my head is clear; and many of my old-age complaints simply vaporized. Blood tests during my annual physical in October confirmed that I had also substantially lowered my cholesterol numbers for the first time in years.

Heart, Mind, and Body

The New Testament assumes that heart, mind, and body are inter-related parts of an undivided, unified whole often described as Hebrew anthropology. The alternative is Greek anthropology where heart, mind, and body operate independently.

Why did Jesus need to experience bodily resurrection after the crucifixion? Jesus was not a ghost, that is, a spirit without a body, and he was not a zombie, a body without a spirit. Jesus rose from the dead—re-created whole—retaining physical scars. However, Jesus displayed no emotional scars, as might be expected of someone resuscitated after having been tortured. Bodily resurrection exemplifies Hebrew anthropology because heart, mind, and body are interrelated, not separable in a complete, healthy person.

Sunshine and Exercise

I have often been chided for advising depressed people to get more sunshine and exercise, both natural anti-depressants. In my own burnout narrative, this advice worked but only after several months of effort.

Other than recognizing the importance of Hebrew anthropology, the spiritual principle at work here is that pain presents us with a Gethsemane moment. In our pain, do we turn to God and give it over to him or do we turn into our pain and hold a pity-party? (Matt 26:39) Elsewhere, Jesus says plainly "Whoever does not take his cross and follow me is not worthy of me." (Matt 10:38)

In a world of chronic problems and endless ways to avoid pain, this teaching sounds harsh. Many friends and family members, when hearing of my burnout, have often advised me to find a good counselor or simply to get my doctor to prescribe anti-depressants. Is sunshine and exercise a harsh response? Yes, it is harsh, almost masochistic. But if God communicates with us through our pain and we medicate our way through it, what have we learned and how has the experience transformed us?

As the Apostle Paul suggested in Romans 5:3–4 cited above, how we respond to our Gethsemane moments ultimately defines who we are as Christians.

Transcendence and Identity

> *Let us make man in our image,*
> *after our likeness . . .*
> *So God created man in his own image,*
> *in the image of God he created him;*
> *male and female he created them.*
> (Gen 1:26–27)

For us as Christians, our identity is secure—we are created in the image of God. If you want to know who you are, look at Jesus, our role model and God's son. As I have said previously, Jesus is my denominator—the measure of all things human.

So why the recent obsession with identity?

Part of the issue of identity is a uniquely modern and postmodern phenomena. For most of the last ten thousand years, our societal role, hence identity, was limited and fixed by family roles, the agrarian community in which one lived, and one's religion. For the urban dweller today, nothing is fixed—not family roles, not community participation, not religious confession. Every aspect of life is up for grabs. If every source of stability is removed, the question of identity is an ever-present preoccupation (Fukuyama 2018, 35).

Theologically, if God the father seems illusive and Jesus is just a man, then the whole denominator analogy falls apart. The fascination in the identity question is a mirror image of God's evaporating transcendence in the American mindset. The implication is that if God is not real, neither are we—our identity is lost.

The Problem of Dysfunction

Being created in the image of God (Gen 1:27) may sound quaint to postmodern ears, but it becomes terribly important in understanding the implications of idolatry, the worship of images other than God. Think of idolatry as a hierarchy of priorities.

The First Commandment makes this point: "You shall have no other gods before me." (Exod 20:3) The Second Commandment reinforces the point of the first one (Exod 20:4–6). Centering our living on the one who made us gives life meaning and stability. Not doing so, leads to dysfunction. Our number-one priority is effectively our god (Hoekema 1994, 84). If God is not our number-one priority, we commit the sin of idolatry.

Idolatry and Priorities

The focus on carved images recalls pagan temple worship, as the Psalmist makes light of:

> Our God is in the heavens; he does all that he pleases. Their idols are silver and gold, the work of human hands. They have mouths, but do not speak; eyes, but do not see. They have ears, but do not hear; noses, but do not smell. They have hands, but do not feel; feet, but do not walk; and they do not make a sound in their throat. Those who make them become like them; so do all who trust in them. (Ps 115:3–8)

The key verse here is the last one: "Those who make them become like them." Image theology implies that we become like the god that we worship, even if we worship idols. Giglio (2003, 13) writes:

> So how do you know where and what you worship? It's easy. You simply follow the trail of your time, your affection, your energy, your money, and your loyalty. At the end of that trail you'll find a throne; and whatever, or whoever, is on that throne is what's of highest value to you. On that throne is what you worship.

Idol worship threatens our identity because over time we become like the god that we worship.

Idolatry Hampers Spiritual Formation

How much time do you spend each week in activities contributing to your spiritual formation as compared with other activities? Intensive activities form us and become part of our identity—spiritual formation is not the only formation that takes place.

Many men spend much of their free time in shoot-them-up video games, often developed by the armed forces for training soldiers. Is it any wonder that, in spite of the fact that automatic weapons have been available since the 1920s, it is only in the last decade that we have seen a rise in mass shootings in public places in the United States unrelated to any political or economic agenda?

Poor formation leads us to worship idols that mislead and let us down. When our idols crash, we experience an existential crisis because we must completely reorganize our priorities (Hos 8:4).

The Problem of Suicide

Consider what happens if your number-one priority is work and you lose your job. In spite of record low unemployment, anxiety, depression, drug addiction, and suicide are at record levels in the United States, and have contributed to a decline in life expectancy (Bernstein 2018).

Amidst the high level of suicide (Tavernise 2016), two age groups stand out: Young people under the age of thirty and older white men, a group not historically prone to suicide. Among young people, the typically reason for attempting suicide is a broken relationship (idolizing a person); among older men, the typical reason is a lost job (idolizing work).

Death by suicide is just the tip of the iceberg.

Based on large national surveys, for every fourteen suicides per hundred thousand people each year, approximately five hundred people attempt suicide and three thousand think about it (Mason 2014, 28).

If psychiatric problems, such as addictions, anxiety, and depression, have a spiritual root, then talk therapy and medication only ease the pain; they do not solve the problem. A solution requires dealing with the root causes, like idolatry and malformation (May 1988, 14–16).

God's Love

Because we are created in the image of God and are commanded to love him and only him, God's jealousy is part of his care for us. The Jewish daily prayer, known in Hebrew as the *Shema* (the name), goes like this:

> Hear, O Israel: The LORD our God, the LORD is one. You shall love the LORD your God with all your heart and with all your soul and with all your might. (Deut 6:4–5)

Loving God above all else vaccinates us from some serious problems.

Reclaiming Lost Transcendence

The problem of lost transcendence arises because the world screams at us and attempts to drown out the still, small voice of God. Although God has created us, and, in sending Jesus Christ to die for ours, has saved us, we need to make room in our lives—both mind and body—to hear God's voice.

The whole point of the spiritual disciplines is to find space in our lives for God. It is possible to "fake it until you make it" with spiritual disciplines, but because God stands outside of time and space—he can approach us but we, being limited in time and space, cannot bridge the gap on our own. Bridging the gap is the work of Christ.

Our faith in Christ gives us the strength to pursue the spiritual disciplines. The Apostle Paul writes: "If you confess with your mouth that Jesus is Lord and believe in your heart that God raised him from the dead, you will be saved." (Rom 10:9) When we express faith in this way, the Holy Spirit enters our hearts and bridges the gap through faith in Jesus Christ. Transcendence becomes a reality when we experience salvation and we find a firm identity in Christ.

COMMUNITY

The Bible takes words seriously, yet the God of the Bible does not prefer any particular human language. The church could be defined as a community where people listen both to one another and to God. Listening is important because ethics requires interpretation of the Bible and of events under the guidance of the Holy Spirit. The church also should shelter the entire community, especially widows, orphans, and immigrants, during economic hardship.

Moses' Call

> *And the angel of the LORD appeared to him in a flame of fire out of the midst of a bush. He looked, and behold, the bush was burning, yet it was not consumed.* (Exod 3:2)

The story of Moses' encounter with God in the burning bush poses a natural Rorschach test. What do we learn?

We learn is that God is present, available, and calling Moses into relationship and Moses responds to God's call (Exod 3:4). Where God is, is holy ground (Exod 3:5). When God identifies himself, Moses responds in fear (Exod 3:6). God reads Moses' deepest desire of his heart and acknowledges the suffering of his people in Egypt (Exod 3:7). God commissions Moses to deliver the people from Pharaoh (Exod 3:10). Moses again responds with fear (Exod 3:11).

God first created in Moses a desire to free his people and then God called on Moses to step up and honor his own desire. While the burning bush served as a Rorschach test, it did not project Moses' attributes on God.

Rather, God used the burning bush to teach Moses about himself, making plain Moses' own desires. The ultimate consequence was the establishment of the nation of Israel.

Interpretative Community

The interpretative problem in ethics arises because every observer of an action may explain it differently. While seminary students are instructed in biblical interpretation, the ethical problem is seldom discussed and formal training, if provided, is handled as an apprentice activity. Biblical interpretation is easier because the interpretative context is fixed and can usually be described. Ethical interpretation is harder because each observer brings their own cultural and philosophical context, which may only be partially understood.

The Interpretation Problem

Let's return for a moment to our shooting example.

The interpretative problem in ethics is complex enough that even experienced judges can get it wrong. Suppose one man shoots another. Immediately, everyone wants to know details of what happened. Consider these questions:

- Who were the men?
- What were their ethnicities?
- What was their relationship?

- What roles did they play?
- What was going on at the time of the shooting?
- Has this happened before?
- What was the motivation for the shooting?

Suppose a judge officiates the trial and the jury finds the shooter innocent (or guilty). What happens if the community riots when the decision is announced? In the case of a shooting, emotions may run wild, but every action poses similar interpretational challenges.

The Church as an Interpretative Community

The community plays an important role in interpretation. For Christians, the pertinent community is the church, but the church's interpretative role arises primarily in teaching. The final word in interpreting events rests mostly with the state, although the media increasingly plays a significant role. When the church abdicates its interpretative role, the state both determines and polices morality.

Key Role of the Bible

The Bible is a book written by adults for adults, yet as biblical illiteracy grows it is increasing obvious that the modern church treats the Bible as a book written for kids. Consider these observations:

- Sunday school attendance is weak, particularly among adults.

- The primary entry point to ministry in many churches is youth group leadership, but churches often recruit young pastors with little life experience or biblical awareness.

- Sermons have grown shorter, often feature feel-good topics, and seldom ask listeners to learn or do anything.

- When the Bible is neglected, spiritual disciplines tend to emphasize spiritual experiences rather than opening us up to receive God's word for our lives and acting on it.

As biblical illiteracy within the church grows, the void created is filled by other things. Instead of pointing people to God, the church increasingly uses the scarce time available to serve as an interpretative community for particular ethnic groups, economic classes, or gender identities. This, of course, leads to greater illiteracy and division within the church.

Cultural Context

*M*ost of our discussion up to this point has focused on individual behavior and learning, but no one is an island—even Robinson Crusoe was never truly alone before he met Friday (DeFoe 1719). We live and participate in the cultures of our families, workplace, and society that influence our thinking, language, and behavior directly through rules, regulations, and law, and indirectly by structuring the presuppositions that we use in all our decisions.

What is Culture?

Culture is term taken from sociology that is often described as the sum of a society's traditions, especially as they pertain to literature, the arts, language, and music. A more helpful framework, however, can be built based on decision requirements in a corporate context. Far from irrelevant to spiritual formation, work culture plays a key role in secular formation.

Nobel laureate economist Herbert Simon defined rationality as making a choice among all possible alternatives. Economists more generally hypothesize that the firm strives to maximize its net present value assuming perfect knowledge of all future cash flows. This implies that the firm works to earn as much as it can, today and in the future. If all decisions are rational and predictable given knowledge about technology and market prices, this theory implies that a firm has no culture because given a set of circumstances, every manager would reach the same decision.

In practice, we observe that decisions are costly, resources are limited, and decisions are frequently made based on rules of thumb and habit. For these reasons, Simon extended the theory of the firm to limit rational behavior—his theory of bounded rationality (Simon 1997, 88). Culture arises because rational decisions are costly. Managers ration their time by applying rules of thumb based on previous decisions and known costs and benefits, not perfect information. These rules of thumb plus manager training and experience determine a firm's decision culture. Interestingly, the costlier rational decisions are, the stronger the cultural effect.

Culture is more sensitive to failures than successes because failures cost more. When an investment succeeds, the investment is returned and a profit is generated, but when an investment fails, the investment is lost and even more losses are possible.

This observation also applies to individuals. Jung (1955, 57) observes:

> But the psychotherapist learns little or nothing from his successes. They mainly confirm him in his mistakes, while his failures, on the other hand, are priceless experiences in that they not only open up the way to a deeper truth, but force him to change his views and methods.

The point is that both individuals and firms need to learn from their mistakes and failures. Healthy organizations promote constructive dialogue about both project successes and failures (Stanton 2012, 10).

The existence of culture makes a firm's history interesting. The time sequence of decisions and their consequences predisposes the organization toward some growth paths and away from others, a concept described as path-dependence. The personal histories of leaders are also important in determining the speed at which decisions are made because hiring expertise is often cheaper than acquiring it directly through experience.

Cultural Personality Types

The existence of culture suggests why organizations develop classifiable cultural personalities. Criteria describing these types include preferred decision style, key values, primary mode for training, nature of control process, and default transaction-opportunity cost trade-off. A culture articulates key values in terms of where decisions ideally take place.

Three cultural archetypes stand out today that compete for dominance: A traditional culture, a modern culture, and a postmodern culture. A fourth type, a dying culture (or culture under stress) is more of a transition phase than a stable culture.

At any time, subcultures within society may favor any one of these types. Competition among these types is influenced by the resources available and other environmental circumstances beyond immediate control. This suggests why a subculture can rise in dominance and dominance can also pass back and forth between subcultures. Progress from one to another is neither inevitable or expected because circumstances external to the firm may dictate the ideal culture (Hiemstra 2009).

The Types

A modern culture delegates authority to line managers, whose technical competence informs objective decisions. A postmodern culture shares decision authority to assure that decisions are equitable. A traditional culture centralizes many decisions to adhere to senior management preferences and value primarily loyalty. Training and control processes reinforce these cultural preferences.

A dying organization is an organization in crisis. A dying organization may start with any cultural affinity but evolves toward a traditional culture. This is because crises consist of a rapid series of nonstandard problems that exceed delegations and require senior management input. Cutbacks likewise strengthen the position of senior managers.

The mix of transaction costs and opportunity costs also reflects cultural affinities. Transaction costs rise with the number of people participating in decisions, while opportunity costs (the cost of not choosing the next best alternative) rise as decision alternatives are excluded. The traditional culture has the lowest transaction costs because it considers the fewest options—only senior manager preferences are consulted. The postmodern culture consults the most people, but it is not particularly reflective—only options actively advocated are considered. Transaction costs in the modern culture fall between these two extremes, but the modern culture prefers a review of all options.

Williamson (1981, 1564) sees both organizational costs constrained by market prices, suggesting that cultures evolve to reflect competitive conditions in the markets served. The dominant culture type may evolve with both market pressures and leadership changes, which may over time lead to overlapping cultural attributes.

An office evolving from a modern to a postmodern type, for example, may begin to exhibit more group decision making, place less emphasis on academic credentials in assignments and promotions, and rely less on peer review of work products. As Alchian (1950) argues, the learning process is likely a combination of trial and error, imitation of successful firms, and deliberative planning because uncertainty makes it unlikely that future market conditions can be fully anticipated.

Behavioral Weaknesses Impede Learning

Cultural types describe attributes at a point in time, while changing circumstances may force organizations to learn and adapt. Learning behavior is therefore a key measure of risk management performance. We observe behavior problems when incentive structures disrupt normal learning processes, create logical traps, or exacerbate normal organizational inertia.

An organizational culture mirrors its environment because decisions and rules evolve over time to deal with environmental challenges. Rewards of money, power, and status within an organization accrue to leaders that facilitate this evolution. When prior decisions and rules need to change, a conflict arises because those changes may threaten the social position of those leaders.

Consider the case of a firm in a growing business. Suppose the firm starts out as a specialized firm in a competitive market. As it grows and acquires competitors, it takes market prices as given. However, as market share grows it eventually becomes the market and can set the price, which favors evolution to a postmodern culture. Further growth requires that it diversify into new markets. At each stage in the firm's growth, the rules for success and risks change (Porter 1980, 191–295). If the organizational culture adapts with a lag and a threat grows quickly enough, firm solvency could be threatened before adaptation is complete.

Christian Culture

Although the Christian faith encourages rational decisions, Christian culture differs from these types because the objective of Christian culture is conformity to Christ, rather than conformity to the rational model. Still, the above cultural types influence how dominations are governed.

The term *polity* refers to how a denomination or church is governed. A denomination managed by bishops is likely organized with a traditional culture, while a church managed through direct voting by the congregation likely has a postmodern culture. Meanwhile, a church managed by elders and professionally trained clergy likely has a modern culture. Each of these polities can operate differently in practice, but the formal structure of the polity clearly shapes the culture of churches and denominations.

Just like no perfectly rational firms exist, Christians

cannot obtain perfection in this life. Yet, Christ is our sacred North Pole, and we have the Holy Spirit to guide us. With our compass set on north, we are not easily led into darkness but focus on the light. Through the inspiration of the Holy Spirit, we normally avoid logical traps and quickly repent when we fall into one. In Christ we have the perfect guidance system even when our lives are not perfect.

Language

> *And God said, let there be light,*
> *and there was light.* (Gen 1:3)

The Bible takes words seriously. God uses words to create the universe. The Apostle John equates these words with the pre-immanent Christ:

> In the beginning was the Word, and the Word was with God, and the Word was God. He was in the beginning with God. All things were made through him, and without him was not anything made that was made. (John 1:1–3)

The original Greek of this passage uses the word *logos* which translates into the noun *word* in English, but in Latin and in modern Spanish *logos* is translated as the *verb*, which emphasizes the action implied in this word.

The seriousness of words is highlighted elsewhere in the Bible. In Genesis, Jacob tricks his father into giving him his brother's blessing, but when his deception is discovered, his father refused to take back the blessing (Gen 27:35). In Exodus, two of the Ten Commandments in the Mosaic covenant govern proper speech: Taking the Lord's name in vain and bearing false witness (Exod 20: 7,

16). Numerous times in the Gospels, Jesus heals and casts out demons with nothing other than verbal commands (e.g. Mark 5:13).

Pentecost Reverses Babel's Curse

The importance of language in the formation of communities is highlighted in the Tower of Babel narrative, as we read:

> Now the whole earth had one language and the same words. And as people migrated from the east, they found a plain in the land of Shinar and settled there. And they said to one another, Come, let us make bricks, and burn them thoroughly. And they had brick for stone, and bitumen for mortar. Then they said, Come, let us build ourselves a city and a tower with its top in the heavens, and let us make a name for ourselves, lest we be dispersed over the face of the whole earth. (Gen 11:1–4)

Here the establishment of Babel is explicitly linked to a common language. These people were proud, wanting to make a name for themselves, and they rebelled against the divine commandment to "Be fruitful and multiply and fill the earth and subdue it." (Gen 1:28) Because of their malformation, God cursed them to be confused by language and thereby forced them to disperse as commanded earlier (Gen 11:7–9).

Fast forwarding to the New Testament, the giving of the Holy Spirit on Pentecost occurred in this way:

> When the day of Pentecost arrived, they [the disciples] were all together in one place. And suddenly there came from heaven a sound like a mighty rushing wind, and it filled the entire house where they were sitting. And divided tongues as of fire appeared to them and rested on each one of them. And they were all filled with the Holy Spirit and began to speak in other tongues [languages] as the Spirit gave them utterance. (Acts 2:1–4)

Pentecost is celebrated today as the birth of the Christian church. Whereas language differences divided people in the Tower of Babel narrative, the Holy Spirit's gift of understanding and speaking different languages unites people and forms the church.

Christian Culture

Christianity does not assert that God prefers any particular human language. The Old Testament was written mostly in Hebrew and the New Testament was exclusively written in Greek, but the Bible has been translated into more languages (about 700) than a person can name. The language of the church is our understanding and worship of God, not the speaking of any particular language.

The church's support for literacy and education helped develop many modern languages, such as English and German, as the Bible was translated into local dialects—a tangible legacy of Pentecost. Left to themselves, most languages fragment along class and ethnic lines, leading to greater divisions and conflict. Likewise, national cultures fragment into subcultures and lose their cohesion with the development of slang.

The idea that postmodern culture is superior to Christian culture because of new cultural insights suggests a lack of insight into the history of the church. Because Christian culture is truly transnational, multicultural, multiethnic, and transracial, the Christian message needs to be expressed in culturally sensitive language, but need not be fundamentally changed to accommodate any particular culture. Quite the contrary, as children of a common Heavenly Father, the church brings people together and helps them understand each other in spite of linguistic differences.

The Language of Faith

One of the most important spiritual breakthroughs that I experienced in seminary arose because I found myself surrounded by biblically articulate and emotionally intelligent students and faculty. My spiritual walk accelerated because I suddenly found the words to express my feelings, emotions, relationships, and theological ideas and to understand the role that God played in my own life. If God can forgive my sins, perhaps I can forgive those annoy and hurt me. Words I already knew took on new meaning as I associated these words with stories from the Bible and ministry experiences.

Given this new vocabulary, I experienced life more fully. For example, take the concept of a boundary from psychology. If our identities are more solidly expressed when we honor and defend our personal boundaries, we gain a sense of security—the shalom (peace) of God. Life is simpler when we know who we are and who we are not. When we take this concept of a boundary and apply it to the Bible's teaching on morality, this peace extends even deeper into our identity.

Take the Hebrew word *shalom*, which means a sense of peace, wholeness, and security. Knowing *shalom* means more than simply the absence of conflict, as inferred by the English word *peace*, opens up new horizons. I am no longer content with an absence of conflict because I truly desire *shalom* in my personal and communal life, and I become a different person. I may have previously hoped for more in life than simply the absence of conflict, but being unable to express the concept of *shalom* posed an intangible limit to my personal growth.

Understanding *shalom* gives new meaning to the words of the Apostle Paul:

> I appeal to you therefore, brothers, by the mercies of God, to present your bodies as a living sacrifice, holy and acceptable to God, which is your spiritual worship. Do not be conformed to this world, but be transformed by the renewal of your mind, that by testing you may discern what is the will of God, what is good and acceptable and perfect. (Rom 12:1-2)

The church is transformational when it extends the language of faith.

Dialogue

Often God speaks to us through the people around us. Each and every human has intrinsic value in the eyes of God. Between the hint of the divine and this intrinsic value, everyone has an interesting story to tell (Benner 1998, 21).

Dialogue in Writing

Author James Scott Bell described dialogue as "compression and extension of action" because "every word, every phrase that comes out of a character's mouth is uttered because the character hopes it will further a purpose." Every character has an agenda, which makes dialogue a natural forum for conflict (Bell 2014, 12–13).

Bell (2014, 22) sees five functions to dialogue: Describing story information, revealing character, expressing the tone, illustrating the scene, and outlining the theme. How people talk reveals their character in terms of education, social position, regional background, and peer groups (Bell 2014, 35–36).

Why go through all these writing tips about dialogue? When we listen to each other and to ourselves, much can be learned that might not be discovered any other way.

Dialogue in Business

Corporate lawyer Thomas Stanton (2012, 10) writes:

> One of the critical distinctive factors between successful and unsuccessful firms in the crisis was their application of what this book calls constructive dialogue. Successful firms managed to create productive and constructive tension between (1) those who wanted to do deals, or offer certain financial products and services, and (2) those in the firm who were responsible for limited risk exposure.

The importance of quality dialog within an organization arises because no single individual, no matter how bright or experienced, could understand the totality of the highly technical financial environment that now exists. Having an open-minded executive is insufficient; the firm culture must embrace active learning and open communication to thrive and reach its potential.

Context for Dialogue

Most dialogue is transactional because even when we disagree, we both have a stake in talking and are willing to reconcile our differences. This does not imply that the discussion will be easy, but the outcome is presumably open-ended.

The authors of *Crucial Conversations*, cited earlier, break dialog into four stages: Presenting facts (see and hear), telling a story, feeling, and acting. Once emotions take over, actions get locked in. The formation of productive stories channels dialog towards useful action and provides an important entry point in group problem-solving.

Many stories can be told, but not all comport well with the facts or are organizationally helpful. Three kinds of unproductive stories—victim, villain, and helpless stories—arise that are usually counter-productive (PGMS 2012, 116–119). These three unproductive stories serve to deflect responsibility for solving group problems and to absolve those advancing such stories from helping turn things around.

Good Dialogue is Rare

If dialogue is important in caring for people, in communication, and in risk management in a corporate setting, why has good dialogue become so rare? These days we are used to commentators and politicians shouting at each on television with virtually no one listening. We are also accustomed to interactions on social media that share information not expecting a response and, if one is given, the person responding is often de-friended when differences arise.

Why have our egos become so fragile that we cannot hear anyone providing an alternative view? There is actually a word for this fragile-ego syndrome: Micro-aggression. A micro-aggression is a subtle, indirect, or unintentional slight, like not paying enough attention to all members of a group. When it is hard to hear information inconsistent with someone's self-image or preconceptions of an issue, dialogue dies.

A Biblical Example

In Matthew's Gospel, Jesus exhorts us to be reconciled with our neighbors before going to church to worship. The example he gives is of a man who has failed to pay his debts. Jesus says:

> Come to terms quickly with your accuser while you are going with him to court, lest your accuser hand you over to the judge, and the judge to the guard, and you be put in prison. (Matt 5:25)

In today's context, a debtor unable to repay a loan for reasons like illness or unemployment can often negotiate with their lender to extend payments or make less than full payment. However, the debtor must be willing to talk with the lender. If debtors refuse to speak with the lender, they are more likely to evicted or slapped with a fine.

Dialogue as Community

Community is a place where people listen to one another respectfully. The church could be defined as a community where people listen both to one another and to God. Making this dialogue a reality is the purpose of church confessions and polity rules that have presumably been drafted under the inspiration of scripture and the Holy Spirit.

Church and State Up Until the Reformation

The relationship between church and state defines the cultural boundaries on religious life and practices. One of the defining characteristics of religious expression in our times is the growth of state power relative to the church. Ironically, the earliest mention of relationship between church and state is the reference to religious persecution, as with Jesus' suffering under Pontius Pilate cited in the Nicene and Apostle's Creeds (PCUSA 1999, 1.2 and 2.2)'.

Today when we talk about our freedom in Christ, we normally refer to our freedom to live within the will of God through Christ's forgiveness and the work of the Holy Spirit. In the early church, freedom in Christ also meant freedom from the micro-management of daily life proscribed by Mosaic Law, which served as the foundation for the theocratic state of Israel.

Church and State in the Bible

Two traditions of church and state relations appear in scripture: The theocratic state of Israel and the magisterium of Rome. The theocratic state of Israel is most obvious in the Old Testament where we observe tension between king and prophet, but this is also the world into which Jesus was born. When Jesus taught about taxation with a denarius coin—render to Caesar the things that are Caesar's, and to God the things that are God's (Matt 22:21)—his concern was that the religious state—even as a client state of Rome—dominated public life to the exclusion of God.

The early persecution of the church, like that of Jesus himself, had a Jewish origin. Before he became Paul the Apostle, Saul was a zealous Jew and persecutor of the church (Acts 8:1–3). Rome allowed Israel autonomy in religious affairs and focused on economic and political matters.

The Apostle Paul, whose ministry was outside the nation of Israel, viewed the state as having more limited influence—that of a civil magistrate—which relieved much of the tension found in Jesus' ministry. Paul exhorts us:

> Let every person be subject to the governing authorities. For there is no authority except from God, and those that exist have been instituted by God. (Rom 13:1)

Paul could travel the Roman Empire establishing churches—frequently over the objection of his Jewish colleagues—because civil authorities showed interest in matters of faith only when public order was disturbed. Even in Jerusalem, Paul is able to use his Roman citizenship to garner protection from the magistrates who saved his life from an angry Jewish mob by arresting him (Acts 21–22). For the most part, religion fell in private space in polytheistic Rome even though Rome occasionally persecuted the church after it became more influential.

Augustine, Luther, and Calvin

This dichotomy between the theocratic state of Israel (still subject to Mosaic law) and the magisterial state of Rome (subject mostly to civil law) found in the New Testament reappears in the writing of Augustine's book, *De Civitate Dei* (*The City of God*). Augustine pictured two eschatological cities: The city of God and an earthly city set in opposition. The city of God consists of those who love God rightly and the earthy city consists of those contemptuous of God (Weitman 2009, 236–237).

Building on Augustine's two cities and Paul's magisterial state, Luther divided the world between the

Kingdom of Christ (church) and the Kingdom of the World (secular state), which defined the concept of church and state in reformation thinking (Bainton 1995, 186–187). Because the reformation divided the Protestant Churches from the Catholic Church, this division between church and state was pragmatic giving legitimacy to the German princes who aided Luther in his break from Rome.

Unlike Luther who was almost exclusively a theologian and pastor, Calvin was both a lawyer and civil magistrate. Calvin's writing on church and state accordingly lent further credibility to Luther's teaching on separation of church and state (Calvin 1939, 202–214). We think of Calvin primarily as a theologian, but he is best known in Europe for having been the first to introduce public education and public water works.

Why Do We Care?

One observation that we can draw from Old Testament law is that it pervades all aspects of daily life. This is the nature of using rules verses principles. Principles can be outlined and applied in an infinite number of contexts; rules always to be updated constantly to deal with new circumstances. Secular law is no different.

Ethical behavior defined in secular law binds every Christian and yet the law need not comport with Christian ethical principles. Christians find themselves in an ethical bind with secular laws that legalize immoral behavior. For parents, it can be difficult explaining to your children that the things their friends are allowed to do, they cannot do because they are Christians. As teenagers, the temptation just to walk away from the faith can be real and immediate.

The breakdown of the separation of church and state means that churches no longer govern the morality of their own members. Church discipline no longer can be applied even to their own members when they are unfaithful to biblical and confessional teaching because membership is voluntary. Only in the case of clergy does the church retain serious influence beyond the reaches of secular law, which increasingly has the intrusive characteristics of Mosaic Law.

Church and State Since the Reformation

The relationship between church and state evolved during the history of the Protestant Churches as reflected in the reformation confessions. The reformation confessions recognize tension between church and state, but argue for separation of the secular and religious domains following Luther.

In the twentieth-century confessions, the old separation of the church and state is clearly breaking down with the increasing power of the state relative to the church and increasing secularization of society. The twentieth-century confessions themselves reflect a new intrusion by the state designed to redefine the church's role in society.

In the discussion that follows, I focus on the creeds and confessions adopted by the Presbyterian Church (USA).

The Early Church Creeds

The suffering of Christ under Pontius Pilate is the only overt mention of a relationship between church and state in the Nicene and Apostle's Creeds (PCUSA 1999, 1.1

and 2.1). The persecution is known from scripture but not explained in these creeds (PCUSA 1999, 4.037–4.039). Both creeds use the enigmatic phrase, a holy catholic church, but the need to emphasize the church's unity (catholic) and being set apart (holy) is not explained. It could be read to separate the church from the secular world, including the state, but we are not told explicitly.

The Reformation Confessions

The reformation confessions codified this separation in Luther's distinction between church and state. For example, the Scots Confession reads under the heading the Civil Magistrate:

> We confess and acknowledge that empires . . . are ordained by God's holy ordinance for the manifestation of his own glory and for the good and well-being of all men. We hold that any men who conspire to rebel or to overturn the civil powers, as duly established, are not merely enemies to humanity but rebels against God's will. (PCUSA 1999, 3.24)

Elsewhere we read:

> To honor father, mother, princes, rulers, and superior powers; to love them, to support them, to obey their orders if they are not contrary to the commands of God, to save the lives of the innocent, to repress tyranny,

> to defend the oppressed, to keep our bodies clean and holy, to live in soberness and temperance, to deal justly with all men in word and deed, and, finally, to repress any desire to harm our neighbor, are the good works of the second kind, and these are most pleasing and acceptable to God as he has commanded them himself. (PCUSA 1999, 3.14)

These divisions and relationships were entirely new during this period and remain important because they inspired the relationship between church and state embedded in the U.S. Constitution (Smylie 1996, 57–61).

The reformation confessions are more than political manifestos. Because the protestant churches broke away from the Roman Catholic Church, they needed to develop more comprehensive statements of their beliefs, including statements of metaphysics, epistemology, anthropology, and ethics. The different confessions each cover these topics, but they cover them in different orders. For example, The Scots Confession starts with a description of God (metaphysics), then moves to discuss the creation of humanity (anthropology), followed by sin (ethics), and later by scripture (epistemology; PCUSA 1999, 3.01, 3.02, 3.03, and 3.19).

The Twentieth Century Confessions

The nineteenth century cast a heavy shadow over the twentieth century because the enlightenment was already past its prime. In Russia and later in China, the overtly atheistic philosophy of communism became the official doctrine, leading to persecution of Christians outside of officially sanctioned churches. Belief in God waned in the western nations and the growth of new technologies led to the rise of state power relative to the church.

Official doctrine in the twentieth century still separated church and state, but religious skepticism increasingly limited the influence of the church over public law and private mores. This skepticism included attacks on the metaphysical and epistemological assumptions of the Bible. The twentieth-century confessions accordingly differ from the reformation confessions in that they neglect their metaphysical and epistemological foundations and focus on anthropological and ethical prescriptions. While we might assume they are grounded in the metaphysical and epistemological foundations of the reformation confessions, the twentieth-century confessions stray from theological orthodoxy even in what is said.

The Theological Declaration of Barmen. The growth of National Socialism in Germany in the 1930s led the government of Adolf Hitler to propose an officially sanctioned church of "German Christians" with overt political objectives. Representatives of the Lutheran, Reformed, and United Churches met May 29–31, 1934, and drafted The Theological Declaration of Barmen. Key participants in this confession were pastors Hans Asmussen, Karl Koch, Karl Iraruer, Martin Niemoller, and Karl Barth (PCUSA 1999, 246–247).

The Theological Declaration of Barmen rejects six false doctrines:

1. Holding up other doctrines as of equal importance with God's revelation in scripture.

2. Suggesting that parts of our lives are not subject to the reign of Christ and are subject to other lords.

3. Ordering the doctrine of the church to current ideologies and political convictions.

4. Vesting special powers to leaders who rule over the church.

5. Giving the church absolute control

      over people's lives beyond the church's special commission.

6. Placing the Word of God and the work of the church in their service of any arbitrarily chosen desires, purpose, or plans.

The Theological Declaration of Barmen organized no new churches or other bodies to implement the declaration, but simply asked the churches for prayer and support for participating pastors. With no official power, The Theological Declaration of Barmen attempted to persuade believers and limit the ability of Nazi government to manipulate the church (Barth 1959, 160). With some editing, the Theological Declaration of Barmen could be used to critique similar trends in secular society today.

The Confession of 1967. If the Theological Declaration of Barmen responded to an external threat to the church posed by the State, then The Confession of 1967 responded to an internal threat to the church posed by the encroachment of modern and postmodern culture. While innovative, the confession followed, rather than led, major changes in society, such as Second Vatican Council of the Roman Catholic Church (1962–65) and the Civil Rights Act of 1964.

The Confession of 1967 builds on part of a single verse: "In Christ God was reconciling the world to himself" (2 Cor 5:19). The verse focuses on reconciling the world to God (evangelism), while the confession refocuses on reconciling us to one another (social ministry). In reworking this verse, the confession crafts a four-part mandate for the church:

> In each time and place, there are particular problems and crises through which God calls the church to act . . . discrimination . . . reconciliation . . . ending poverty in a world of abundance . . . anarchy in sexual relationships. (PCUSA 1999, 9.43–9.47)

Nothing is left out. The summary for the confession reads:

> God's redeeming work in Jesus Christ embraces the whole of man's life: social and cultural, economic and political, scientific and technological, individual and corporate. (PCUSA 1999, 9.53)

Meanwhile, the Supreme Court's decision in the *Roe v. Wade* case in 1973 and rule changes increasing the availability of contraceptives intruded deeply into the personal lives of Christians, rendering church interpretation moot. Even further, the *Obergefell v. Hodges* decision in 2015 redefined marriage to include same-sex marriage, causing deep splits within many denominations over how to respond.

The weight of these changes was to establish a precedent whereby the State could intervene into matters previously reserved for the Church. This reversed a consensus about the separation of church and state that had prevailed since the reformation and allowed new voices to be heard on questions of morality that oppose even the participation of the church in public debate. Having overturned the separation that prevailed on matters of moral conduct, the State has increasingly injected itself into church benevolences, personnel policies, property rights, and teaching on sexuality and the family.

A Brief Statement of Faith. The breakdown of the division between church and state established during the reformation appears complete in the merger of the United Presbyterian Church in the United States of America and the Presbyterian Church in the United States in 1983. The merger itself can be seen as an attempt by the church to consolidate influence already lost to postmodern culture.

The newly formed Presbyterian Church (USA) crafted a Brief Statement of Faith consisting of only eighty lines that focused on the humanity of Christ and a stateless world where we stand almost alone as individuals before

God. For example, the confession said:

> In a broken and fearful world, the Spirit gives us courage to pray without ceasing, to witness among all peoples to Christ as Lord and Savior, to unmask idolatries in Church and culture. (PCUSA 1999, 10.4, Lines 65–69)

Here the private work of believers is to deconstruct (unmask) idolatries in the church and culture equally, suggesting that the church itself is suspect in our relationship with God rather than as the chosen instrument of the Holy Spirit.

It is fair to conclude from The Brief Statement of Faith that the separation of church and state assumed since the reformation no longer exists. The culture, acting through the State as a secular religion, has intruded on the private life of faith and brought it into the public domain. The public crusades of The Confession of 1967 have become private crusades in The Brief Statement of Faith.

This perhaps explains the new emphasis in pastoral care and the psychological hermeneutic in ministering to a broken and fearful world as the grand political campaigns of the past have been extinguished. Who today honestly remembers that abolition of slavery, equality of the sexes, public education, and expansion of human rights were once Christian initiatives? (Dayton 2005)

Where Jesus contended with intrusion of Mosaic Law, the Church today contends with an activist, secular State within its very walls, rendering the concept of a division of church and state anachronistic.

Hidden Ministries

Hellerman (2001, 1) asks an intriguing question: What explains "the marked growth of the early Christian movement?" His response is that the early church was a surrogate family that:

> may be defined as a social group whose members related to one another neither by birth nor by marriage, but who nevertheless (a) employ kinship terminology to describe group relationships and (b) expect family-like behavior to characterize interactions among group members. (Hellerman 2001, 2)

Peter used sibling terminology on the Day of Pentecost (Acts 1:16)—before the church had been organized—and Paul used it throughout his writings (e.g. 1 Cor 1:10). Referring to God as father (e.g. Matt 6:9 and John 17:1) is also consistent with the idea that we are all brothers and sisters in the faith. Furthermore, the early church shared resources, acting like a family in taking care of one another (Acts 2:44–45).

Introducing Family Systems

In this context, family systems may hold a key to congregational ministry. Families matter more than conventional wisdom suggests. A death in the family may leave one person with chronic migraine headaches; another may develop back pain or experience a heart attack; a third may exhibit psychiatric dysfunction. A medical doctor or counselor treating only an individual's symptoms may not have a high degree of success because the cause of the symptoms lies in the family system, not the individual.

While pastors and chaplains may not be surprised by this observation, standard medical and counseling training and practices focuses almost exclusively on the individual.

Five Concepts

Friedman (1985, 19) outlines five basic concepts in family systems theory, including:

1. The identified patient;
2. The concept of balance (homeostasis);
3. Differentiation of self;
4. The extended family field; and
5. Emotional triangles.

Each of these concepts deserves discussion.

The Identified Patient. Symptoms arise in a family

system first in the weakest members of the system. This unconscious scapegoating effect arises, in part, because they are least able to cope with problems elsewhere in the system, like plumbing subject to excessive water pressure bursts at the weakness link (Friedman 1985, 21).

For example, a child may act out (nail biting, bed-wetting, fighting in school, teenage troubles, and so on) because the parents have marital difficulties. Focusing on the child may simply make the problem worse, while counseling the parents may not only resolve the marital difficulties, but the child's issue as well.

Balance. The family emotional system strives to maintain equilibrium (resist change) having an effect not unlike a thermostat. When problems surface, questions according arise like: What is out of equilibrium? Why now? Ironically, familiar dysfunction may be preferred to therapeutic change. Dynamic stability may accordingly be attained, in part, by how loosely or tightly individuals respond to changes.

Friedman classifies families as tightly or loosely integrated. Families that are loosely integrated exhibit a greater capacity to absorb stress simply because they are less reactive to the stress. (Friedman 1985, 24–26)

Differentiation of Self. Differentiation means the capacity to be an "I" while remaining connected. Differentiation loosens the integration thereby increasing the shock-absorbing capacity of the system. The ideal here is to remain engaged in the system but in an non-reactive manner—a non-anxious presence. Greater self-differentiation offers the opportunity for the entire system to change by reducing the resistance to change (homeostasis).

Family leaders (including pastors in church families) who develop greater self-differentiation can accordingly bring healing in the face of challenges. This is a principle that can aid leaders in many a dysfunctional organization (Friedman 1985, 27–31).

Extended Family Field. Understanding one's extended family and family history can identify unresolved issues and repeating patterns. The principle is that one cannot solve a family system's problem by withdrawing temporally or geographically—in such events we simply take our issues with us. This is why your thirty-year, high school reunion may be marked by a return of old flames and buried resentments. Such problems have a nasty habit of reappearing, like genetic diseases transmitted by DNA.

Friedman (1985, 32) observes that family trees are always trees of knowledge and often they are also trees of life. This re-emergence of family systems problems across time and distance extends the principle of homeostasis.

Emotional Triangles. Friedman (1985, 35) writes:

> An emotional triangle is formed by any three persons or issues . . . when any two parts of a system become uncomfortable with one another, they will 'triangle in' or focus on a third person, or issue, as a way of stabilizing their own relationship with one another.

This has the effect of putting stress on the third person to balance the system. An unsuspecting pastor could participate in many such triangles and simply burn out. This leads Friedman to observe that stress is less the result of quantitative notion such as "overwork" and more the effect of our position in the triangle of our families.

The importance of the pastor's stance in a church family is obvious in this framework. The pastor functions as a parent in the church family system. Problems in the pastor's family of origin have the potential to transmit into the church family because of the pastor's key role in the system. If the pastor is not a non-anxious presence within the system, then this presence could also bring healing. Homeostasis can leave a new pastor vulnerable to dysfunction in a church years after the apparent source of the problem, perhaps a prior pastor, has left.

Hiddenness

The relative emptiness of church pews may not be a good indicator of the influence of the church and church leaders within the community.

Suppose the only family members to attend church were the over-functioning members. Teaching over-functioning members to become a non-anxious presence, perhaps by modeling Sabbath rest, could bring healing to an entire extended family. The importance of funerals becomes more obvious because members of the extended family may suddenly find themselves in church for the first time in many years.

Alternatively, one might find a young person in the youth program acting out. Viewing the young person as the weak link in the family system may provide a flag for unspoken marital difficulties in the family, either present or absent from church. But how would one know unless the pastor made a house call?

Of course, the church as a family system could also be dysfunctional, refusing to cope with leadership problems that manifest in excessive gossip, pastoral burnout, or disregard for the mission of the church.

Downward Mobility

> *There is neither Jew nor Greek,*
> *there is neither slave nor free,*
> *there is no male and female,*
> *for you are all one in Christ Jesus.*
> (Gal 3:28)

*M*y first ministry involved organizing a summer program for students at my parent's new church home in McLean, Virginia, in the late 1970s. The high school students loved this idea, and I continued to organize the summer program throughout graduate school. Over these years, I saw one cohort of students after another progress through school, graduate, and move away from affluent Northern Virginia, a process that I described as downward mobility.

The Downwardly Mobile

This downward mobility afflicts most young people today. Studies show that real income in the United States has been relatively flat for college graduates since about 1980. The average student has a couple years of college before dropping out and, like high school graduates, has suffered a decline in real income since 1980. Only students with postgraduate work—maybe ten–twenty percent of the population—have seen an increase in real income since 1980, generally associated with their ability to take advantage of changes in information technology—the hamburger helper of today's professionals.

This downward mobility has placed economic pressure on many people, making it hard to purchase a home or have a family. The disappearance of pensions and healthcare plans are related problems. In the midst of this economic pressure, American society has increasingly been stratified by economic class. Throw in gender, race, and ethnicity, and you have a highly combustible mixture because no one feels better off. The decline in life expectancy over the past three years, due in part to record suicides and drug overdoses, is testimony to the stress that people feel.

Being the Church

In the middle of a chaotic social situation and pressure on budgets, how does the church resist the temptation to serve only the wealthier economic classes rather than the entire community?

Churches, like the Roman Catholics, that operate on the parish model are better able to serve the entire community than those that differentiate themselves based on their theological heritage, like most Protestant churches. A parish is defined geographically and should ideally serve both rich and poor neighborhoods equally.

A theologically defined church attracts one or another social group, depending on particular concerns. A church promoting the prosperity Gospel, for example, is much more likely to attract the economically-disadvantaged while the work-ethic of traditional Calvinist denominations, like the Presbyterians, is more likely to appeal to professional groups.

Irrespective of structure or theology, we are called as Christians to minister to and evangelize the entire community.

The Problem of Immigration

Massive immigration from Latin American countries, particularly in Central America, has exacerbated class distinctions in America. Hispanic immigrants often speak no English and lack documentation that allows them to work in the United States. Political deadlock has led a humanitarian crisis at the border and the development of a rigid underclass in virtually every American city.

Policy changes in the United States helped promote this immigration. Most obvious is U.S. drug policy as illegal drug use in America has prompted the growth of narco-trafficking and the development of drug gangs in Central America. Less obvious is the effect of the North American Free Trade Agreement (NAFTA), which lowered the price of grain in Central America, undermining the rural economy after 1994 and prompting out-migration of farm workers. Complicating matters, the lack of population growth in the United States has created an urgent need for workers in low-wage industries, such as janitorial services, hospitality, construction, and agriculture, that has attracted displaced workers.

Role for Churches

While immigration has met the need for workers and promoted economic growth, the Hispanic immigration has proceeded too quickly for immigrants to be legally and socially integrated into American society. This has created an opportunity for churches to assist in resolving both problems.

The biblical mandate to assist immigrants comes from Exodus, where we read:

> You shall not wrong a sojourner or oppress him, for you were sojourners in the land of Egypt. You shall not mistreat any widow or fatherless child. If you do mistreat them, and they cry out to me, I will surely hear their cry. (Exod 22:21–23)

From a practical perspective, about a third of the children in the United States under the age of twenty share a Hispanic background. Another third are minorities. Learning to serve these groups today while the kids are young is an important investment in the future of congregational ministry.

A Worshipping Community

> *Observe the Sabbath day, to keep it holy,
> as the LORD your God commanded you.*
> (Deut 5:12)

The divine origin of the Sabbath is well-attested in scripture. In the Old Testament, it is the only commandment that appears also in the creation account. It is also the longest commandment—an indicator of emphasis. In the New Testament, Jesus refers to himself as the Lord of the Sabbath (Matt 12:8; Luke 6:5) and performs several miracles specifically on the Sabbath.

A Biblical Understanding

A key to understanding Sabbath is found in Hebrews 4 that lists four aspects of rest: Physical rest, weekly Sabbath rest, rest in the Promised Land, and heavenly rest—our return to the Garden of Eden.

Physical rest is underrated by many Christians. Jesus says: "Come to me, all who labor and are heavy laden, and I will give you rest." (Matt 11:28) How are we to love God and love our neighbors when we are physically exhausted? Sabbath rest allows us to build the physical, emotional, and spiritual capacity to experience God and to have compassion for our neighbors.

Sabbath rest is a symbol of our Christian freedom. If we compare the Exodus and Deuteronomy renderings of the Fourth Commandment, we find that Deuteronomy adds the sentence:

> You shall remember that you were a slave in the land of Egypt, and the LORD your God brought you out from there with a mighty hand and an outstretched arm. (Deut 5:15)

Free people rest; slaves work. Sabbath rest is a symbol of our Christian freedom.

The Promised Land, promised rest (Ps 95:11), heaven, and the new Eden (Rev 22:2) all display and reinforce Sabbath imagery. The image of our Divine Shepherd is one who gives heavenly rest: "He makes me lie down in green pastures. He leads me beside still waters." (Ps 23:2) Sadly, this poetic image of rest only seems to come up at funerals.

The 24/7 Culture

Postmodern culture refuses to rest. Sunday is fast becoming just another day where the malls are open and employers seldom offer overtime to those required to work it. So why does Moses insist on honoring the Sabbath?

Under penalty of death (Num 15:32–35), the prohibition on work on the Sabbath provided a cultural alternative to Pharaoh's relentless pursuit of wealth. Brueggemann (2014, xiii–xiv) writes: "YHWH governs as an alternative to Pharaoh, there the restfulness of YHWH effectively counters the restless anxiety of Pharaoh." Sabbath rest appears in the creation accounts because God balances work and rest. Egyptian gods, by contrast, never rested.

By honoring the Sabbath, Moses created room for the Hebrew people to reflect on their lives and on God. Sabbath rest is a gateway to keeping all the other commandments. What if the threat of death from corona virus convinced people to slow down and smell the roses? The Psalmist's writes: *"Be still, and know that I am God."* (Ps 46:10)

Sacrificial Worship

The link between rest and worship goes beyond occurring primarily on Sundays. Marva Dawn (1991, 1) observes: "To worship the Lord is—in the world's eyes—a waste of time . . . the entire reason for our worship is that

God deserves it." To see this link, consider the ancient practice of offering burnt animal offerings in the temple rather than human sacrifices. Consider the account of Aaron during the Golden Calf incident:

> And he received the gold from their hand and fashioned it with a graving tool and made a golden calf. And they said, These are your gods, O Israel, who brought you up out of the land of Egypt! (Exod 32:4)

No doubt Aaron was simply practicing worship in a manner that he had learned in Egypt—worshiping a Golden Calf (think of the Wall Street Bull) could be thought of as an ancient form of the prosperity Gospel!

Because many of these foreign gods were crafted in the form of animals, sacrificing a bull on the alter offered a way for a Jew to demonstrate his allegiance to God, not to foreign gods. For us today, devoting our Sundays to worshipping God is our way of denying the gods of our age by spending time, donating money, and honoring our marriages, things foreign to our culture.

LEADERSHIP

Christian leadership extends our Christian character as we mentor others and it is the most important application of our faith. Our capacity to assume this mentorship role depends on how we care for our own souls. Our pursuit of holiness and our practice of godliness serve in developing our character and making others aware of it.

Part of this practice is caring for those in our own families, especially the young and the elderly. Part of this practice is understanding the context and presuppositions supporting good character. Part of this is being able to assist others in managing difficult transitions in life. Part of this is being able to be the good example that Christ calls us to be. It all starts with manifesting the heart of Christ and applying faith to solving group and community problems.

Self-Care

Christian leaders need to be self-aware and take care of themselves. Self-care is as easy as practicing Sabbath rest (Exod 20:8–11), and its significance arises because tired people can neither love God nor their neighbor (Matt 22:36–40). In a deeper sense, we are obligated to care for ourselves and shun sin because our bodies and minds are a temple for the Holy Spirit (1 Cor 6:19). Still, in spite of the biblical warrant for self-care, Christian leaders are routinely workaholics and stress addicted, suffering burnout to the point of threatening the ongoing viability of their ministries.

Burnout and Temptation

We are most vulnerable to temptation and sin when our bodies and minds are tired. It is ironic that fasting is a spiritual discipline because fasting weakens our resistance to temptation and sin. After his baptism, Jesus was led by the Holy Spirit into the desert where he fasted for forty days and the devil tempted him three times (Luke 4:1–13). Nouwen (2002, 30,53,75) describes these temptations as the leadership challenges to be relevant, popular, and powerful.

Pastoral burnout often leads to sexual misconduct and departure from ministry. Two pastors close to me early in my career likely succumbed to this temptation. One engaged in a homosexual liaison only to lose his marriage, his job, and, later, his life—he died of AIDS. The other divorced his wife and ran away with a woman in the congregation. Both pastors had mentored me for years, so I know that such behavior was not typical or expected, but burnout and stress bring out the worst in a person.

Three Dimensions of Self-care

Crowley and Lodge (2007, 7) make an audacious claim: Over fifty percent of all illness and injuries in the last third of your life can be eliminated by changing your lifestyle to include regular, strenuous exercise including resistance training. What is regular? At least six days a week. What is strenuous? Exercise able to provide an aerobic effect. What is resistance training? They recommend a program of weight lifting. If you follow their advice, then you can remain like a physically fit, fifty-year old well past the age of 80.

Following Crowley and Lodge, three things were

needed for a successful retirement: Physical activity, mental stimulation, and connection. For seniors, these three things are needed to live a normally, healthy life. They are just as necessary for a healthy life at younger ages, but normally younger people have greater reserves than seniors. Unhealthy lifestyles can cut into reserves at any eighty.

Physical Activity. Routine, strenuous exercise builds physical capacity by enhancing blood flow, reducing fat, and curbing appetite. It also builds mental capacity and increases self-esteem. Even moderate physical activity, such walking with your spouse in the evening, can have a positive impact on attitude and physical fitness.

The impact of physical fitness on mental agility is directly observable in older people. Sunset dementia is a condition where seniors are able to remember things and manage life easily during the day but as the afternoon and evening approaches they begin suffering forgetfulness not observed earlier in the day. The condition is perhaps analogous to a younger person drinking a couple beers or suffering sleep deprivation over multiple days in terms of the lost mental capability.

In my own case, appetite is often the best indicator of my physical and mental well-being. When I am tired, I eat too much and skimp on my exercise routine. If this goes on too long, I put on extra pounds.

Mental Stimulation. Physical activity has a direct, beneficial effect on mental agility. Exercise cleans the plaque out of your veins and widens them, increasing oxygen flow. This is especially important for mental condition because the brain is the single, largest user of blood flow in the body. The more oxygen available to the brain, the clearer our thinking.

The relationship between physical fitness and mentality agility became obvious to me when I was a foreign exchange student for a year in Germany. Germans love to drink beer and play chess so I spent my evenings in local bars playing chess, drinking beer, and practicing my German—sober I was too shy to speak up. After several months of drinking beer and playing chess daily, I was unbeatable, but only for the first two to three hours of play. After three hours of playing chess, even chess rookies could beat me, so I learned to quit after two hours of play.

Beyond physical exercise, the mind also needs

a workout. The brain is a physical organ that atrophies with inactivity just like a muscle. In kids under six years old, musical training is known to enhance thinking until much later in life because music employs the entire brain. For the rest of us, mental exercises, like learning new languages or subjects, alters the brain's physical structure, enhancing our abilities in those directions and stimulating other parts of the brain to remain fit. Physical and mental exercise is believed to delay the onset of brain diseases, like Alzheimer's, that are otherwise incurable.

Connection. Being socially active is important for older people to avoid loneliness and depression, but it is no less important for younger people. It is well-known among educators that college freshman who find clubs and groups to join are much more likely to make a successful transition to college and avoid dropping out. For seniors, researchers at Duke University (1999) reported:

> A study of nearly 4,000 elderly North Carolinians has found that those who attended religious services every week were 46 percent less likely to die over a six-year period than people who attended less often or not at all, according to researchers at Duke University Medical Center.

While Christians recognize the role of faith in life expectancy, even an atheist will recognize the benefits of having close friends and other people who care for you. Life is simply less stressful when you know that you can share your trials and tribulations with others.

Good Example to Others

For the Christian leader, practicing self-care obviously enhances one's durability in ministry, but it is also important to model a balanced lifestyle.

Postmodern people are more anxious and depressed than most previous generations because they are more likely to be cut-off from traditional society, their families, their faith communities, and the communities that they grew up in. Technology and social media amplify these trends. These sources of stress and others conspire together to produce historically unprecedentedly levels of anxiety, depression, and suicide.

In this context, Christians need together with their leaders to demonstrate what a balanced lifestyle looks like. Who knows? The life you save may be your own.

Holiness

> *For I am the LORD who brought you up*
> *out of the land of Egypt to be your God.*
> *You shall therefore be holy,*
> *for I am holy.*
> (Lev 11:45)

The list of church leaders and high government officials whose careers have tanked due to moral failure seems endless. Factors contributing to these moral failures include changing mores, increasing social conflict, and the ability of social media to document our private lives from birth to death. Today nothing is off the record.

The Role of the Church

The church bears responsibility for the moral failures of its leaders. Factors contributing to this problem include:

1. Some churches no longer teach and practice holiness, relegating that responsibility to families and individuals.

2. In some denominations, theology has divided Law from Gospel, suggesting that the holiness code in the Leviticus no longer applies to the Christian.

3. In some churches, the emphasis on love—loosely defined—is so pervasive that other parts of the Bible are simply neglected.

4. Preaching in many churches simply eschews hard teaching on morality because of permissive attitudes on marriage and sexuality in society more generally.

The traditional teaching of the church is clear on the question of holiness, but many churches no longer accept this teaching.

The watchword for this new teaching comes directly from Jesus' Sermon on the Mount: "Beware of false prophets, who come to you in sheep's clothing but inwardly are ravenous wolves. You will recognize them by their fruits." (Matt 7:15–16) Weak teaching can also lead to bad fruit, resulting in unnecessary brokenness and departures from faith. Clearly, God can use broken pastors and broken churches to advance his kingdom, but we should cling to Christ's mantel as closely as we can and avoid grieving the Holy Spirit (Eph 4:30).

Modesto Manifesto

During an evangelistic campaign in Modesto, California, in 1948, Billy Graham asked his team to list the reasons that evangelists had failed in previous campaigns. Four items topped everyone's list:

1. Excessive interest in money and weak accounting of it.

2. Sexual immorality, especially while on the road.

3. Failing to work closely with and respect local churches.

4. Exaggerating ministry successes (Graham 1997, 127–129).

Among these temptations, sexual immorality stood out as a threat and Graham committed himself to never being alone with any woman other than his wife (the Graham rule). These rules, together known as the Modesto Manifesto, have been picked up by other Christian leaders.

The Role of Christian Leaders

The Beatitudes have a general audience, but they also appear as a kind of commissioning service for disciples, which today would be of special interest to Christian leaders. The Sixth Beatitude focuses on a clean heart—"Honored are the pure in heart"—but, how can I remove the impurities? This is a call for holiness. Jesus provides two methods: Pruning and intensifying.

Prune. Jesus gives us two metaphors of pruning, which means cutting away unnecessary or unwanted growth to make a plant stronger and more fruitful (John 15:2). The first metaphor involves eyes: "If your right eye causes you to sin, tear it out and throw it away." (Matt 5:29) The second metaphor involves hands: "And if your right hand causes you to sin, cut it off and throw it away." (Matt 5:30) In both metaphors, we remove sin from our lives by running.

The eye gouging and hand chopping metaphors could also have been heard by Jesus' audience as a messianic call to arms. When the Prophet Samuel anointed Saul King of Israel, he said to him: "And you shall reign over the people of the LORD and you will save them from the hand of their surrounding enemies." (1 Sam 10:1) Notice the hand metaphor in this charge. Saul's first act as king was to save the besieged city of Jabesh-gilead from an Amorite king whose condition for surrender was: "On this condition I will make a treaty with you, that I gouge out all your right eyes, and thus bring disgrace on all Israel." (1 Sam 11:2)

Jesus' pruning metaphors imply that

sanctification—casting off sin and taking on godliness—is serious business: Eyes and hands are parts of the body—parts of us—that are not easily discarded. If the threat of sin were trivial, then a better analogy might have been to trim your nails or cut your hair. But if sin threatens both our physical and spiritual lives, then amputation becomes an acceptable option.

Intensify. Jesus widens the scope of commandments under the law by drilling into the motivation for breaking them, intensifying the scrutiny given to sin. For example, when Jesus talks about adultery, he focuses on the lustful look that corrupts the heart, not the sinful act that follows. If sin begins in the heart, then sanctification must strive for purity of heart, and not only avoiding sin, but pursuing godliness, as the Apostle Paul writes:

> But that is not the way you learned Christ!—assuming that you have heard about him and were taught in him, as the truth is in Jesus, to put off your old self, which belongs to your former manner of life and is corrupt through deceitful desires, and to be renewed in the spirit of your minds, and to put on the new self, created after the likeness of God in true righteousness and holiness. (Eph 4:20–24)

The likeness of God, of course, refers to the divine image

in creation, as implied in the word, godliness, used by Paul in admonishing Timothy: "Train yourself for godliness" (1 Tim 4:7). We should strive to be a good example to others, taking Jesus Christ as our example.

Generational Reach

> *Honor your father and your mother,*
> *that your days may be long in the land*
> *that the Lord your God is giving you.*
> (Exod 20:12)

After the Trinity, the family is our first small group. The church—the bride of Christ—is the family written large. How we treat our family affects everything else we do, if for no other reason than little eyes are watching.

The family is under severe pressure in our time. About eighty percent of Americans have seen no real increase in income since the 1980s. Fertility rates have fallen below the threshold required to reproduce the current population. Suicide rates are a historically high levels, which, together with drug overdoses and premature deaths due to diabetes, has contributed to an unprecedented decline in life expectancy for the past three years. Meanwhile, the focus on individual rights, social media, video gaming, and cell phones have left many young people socially isolated and fearful of assuming family responsibilities.

Postmodern life wears out families. For couples in their family-raising years, two incomes are required to meet the normal expectations for the American dream—two cars, a house, two-point-one kids, college education, a healthcare plan, and retirement savings. Eldercare competes with childcare for time and money. No one can reasonably be expected to meet these expectations, and many have stopped trying. Couples are delaying marriage, and many prefer to retain a single lifestyle even after marriage, sharing life only with their pets.

In the midst of social chaos, Jesus calls us to live a sacrificial lifestyle. We are encouraged to lead a disciplined work life, manage our resources of time, talents, and money carefully, and care for our kids and parents modeled after Christ under the mentorship of the Holy Spirit. The future belongs to those who live in Christ. Honoring your parents in an age that worships sex and youthfulness is a particularly obvious and righteous testimony.

The Eldercare Journey

For those not yet acquainted with eldercare, it poses a number of challenges that no one can fully meet. For the senior, growing old is experienced as a series of losses in function, physical abilities, and relationships, each of which need to be grieved (Mitchell and Anderson 1983, 35–45). Wherever pain and loss are evident, a grieving process is triggered.

For the caregiver, these losses pose gaps that need to be filled. Stepping up to meet these challenges is hard for caregivers because it presumes a role reversal—the parent suddenly becomes the child and the child assumes a parental role. This role reversal is difficult for both parties, and the reversal may need to be repeated as different issues arise.

Consider driving. For suburbanites, every activity starts with a car trip. Driving is a teenage rite of passage for this very reason. A socially-active senior without a driver's license is suddenly house-bound and must depend on others for transportation. Seniors are reluctant to admit their dependence, and caregivers may not have time to fulfill the need. Oftentimes, seniors only surrender their licenses after an accident because their kids are unwilling to raise the issue. Memory-loss issues only make the driving problem worse.

For all the challenges, eldercare also offers the opportunity for children to spend more time with their parents. Where you once knew your parents as a child, now you get to engage with them more fully as an adult. Eldercare can accordingly be a meaningful and fruitful time.

One of the first things I did when my father came down with Alzheimer's disease was to edit and publish his memoir as a prelude to writing my own. This proved to be a fruitful exercise because it deepened my understanding of him and made it possible to share the memoir with the caregivers hired to care for him. For the caregivers and for me, my father grew from a daily burden to someone deserving of empathy, the way God sees him.

Beyond Default Settings

Striking a balance between structure and change is an important struggle for Christians today. Structure can mean worshipping with our preferred music, theology, or ethnic group while change can mean mixing up any of these things. This tension between structure and change exists in all aspects of life today—family, community, church, and work—which exhausts us constantly. Finding peace in the midst of this chaos is a theme in the postmodern church.

Reverting to Default Settings

In the midst of chaos and the absence of reflection, many people and churches naturally revert to their default settings, which often reflect a happy period in their past. In the political realm, we see ethnically-based groups forming that resist compromise and shamelessly promote their own narrow interests. In the church, we see spirited food-fights—worship wars—over small changes in musical genre. These default settings are deeply ingrained aspects of our identity that, as Christians, are supposed to be in Christ, not other things.

At least, three explanations can be offered for these reversions:

1. In a period of fundamental change in life in society, we may look for structure in our Christian lives that previously may have been vested elsewhere.

2. If our faith is not centered on Christ but on other things, then the superficiality of our faith has been unmasked for all to see.

3. It is amazing how often default settings come into play when people act out of fear or anger.

These explanations may also work together to intensify the emotions driving these reversions.

The Role of Presuppositions

Default settings often operate at a subconscious (or presuppositional) level. In its simplest form, a presupposition is an implicit, unstated assumption about how things work. Do you, for example, accept or reject the possibility that the miracles recorded in scripture happened? Modernists assume that miracles cannot take place, while postmoderns no longer accept this presumption (Keener 2003, 266).

Think about the colors, white and black. We

normally associate white with day—a safe time when you can see everything—and black with night—a fearful time when crooks and evil spirits are at work. White is often thought to good, as in the good cowboys wear white hats, while the bad ones wear black hats. Old movies may have even reinforced these cowboy stereotypes, which may seem harmless until we start talking about race relations.

Because presuppositions operate subconsciously, they can affect our behavior without us even being conscious of it. In my own case, I volunteer with Hispanic ministry and often practice my Spanish by listening to Spanish Christian music. Sitting at a traffic light one day, I became anxious about having the windows down as I played my music. Why was I anxious? I was afraid strangers would assume I was Hispanic. Ouch! My subconscious hypocrisy shamed me.

The only way to overcome such presuppositions is to examine our own behaviors and ask: Why am I doing this? Presuppositions stop influencing our behavior when we take the time to reflect on why we impulsively do things.

Emotional Clues

Our emotions often reveal our presuppositions. What makes you mad? Anger always has an object.

Lester (2007, 14) observes that we get angry when we feel threatened. While we could be angry because of a physical threat, most often we get angry because of psychological threats: Threats to our values, our beliefs about right and wrong, and our expectations about the way good people should act. When threatened the intensity of our response depends on the amount of personal investment we have in the values, beliefs, and means that are being threatened. Following this threat model of anger, our first responsibility when we get angry is to recognize we feel threatened and to identify the nature of the threat (Lester 2007, 28–29).

What can be mystifying is when you find yourself intensely angry or hurt without knowing exactly why, a phenomenon known as an emotional hijacking. On reflection, an emotional hijacking may reveal a repressed grief or presupposition that offers rare insight into your emotional history. During my internship at Providence Hospital, the head nurse in the emergency department asked me to speak with a young woman who had miscarried. I ministered to her for about ten minutes before she began ministering to me, as I recalled a ungrieved miscarriage my wife and I experienced twenty years prior. The feelings became so intense I broke off my meeting with the woman and spent the next half hour in tears in the chapel.

What Can Christian Leaders Do?

The more we center our lives on Christ, the less likely we are to revert impulsively to default settings. With Christ as our number-one priority and consulting God in prayer when questions arise, we are more likely to reflect on our actions and less likely to act impulsively.

Centering our lives on Christ does not mean suddenly giving up our favorite music, revising our theology, or hanging out with people that make us uncomfortable. What it does mean is that we will not act impulsively when reflection is warranted. It is amazing how quickly secondary things become secondary when we take such things to God in prayer.

Managing Change

Probably the most difficult aspect of leadership is managing change. Change often causes pain that provides an important clue that the status quo may soon be disrupted. Pain forces us to decide—shall I turned into my pain or turn to God? The answer to this question defines our character both as Christians because life is full of pain.

Seeking Guidance

As the Apostle James reminds us: "If any of you lacks wisdom, let him ask God, who gives generously to all without reproach, and it will be given him." (Jas 1:5) Pain poses a need for pain relief, but the need for guidance is almost always more pressing. Guidance is needed to know how to solve problems and to respond to the pain they cause. Left to simmer, pain often turns into negative self-talk, depression, and anger.

Anger can be especially destructive. In coping with anger, Lester (2007, 62) presents a six-step model:

1. Recognize anger;
2. Acknowledge anger;

3. Calm our bodies;

4. Understand why we are threatened;

5. Evaluate the validity of the threat; and

6. Communicate anger appropriately.

Anger is often suppressed and expressed in a devious manner, such as procrastination; actions that frustrate, embarrass or causes others pain; nasty humor; nagging; silence; sexual deviance; and passive-aggressive behavior (Lester 2007, 88–89).

It is more productive to seek God's advice—Lord, why have you brought me to this time and this place?

Tension Between Stewardship and Theology

The problems facing church leaders today seem endless, but one problem stands out: Stewardship. Real wages have been flat for most workers in the United States since the early 1980s with most income gains accruing to the top ten percent of income earners (Desilver 2018). If one combines wage stagnation with declining church attendance, the stewardship problem becomes obvious. Because of the average age of members in many small churches in over sixty, a financial crisis accompanies every funeral. The disproportionately high number of senior deaths with corona virus in 2020 will only exacerbate this problem.

The stewardship crisis facing American churches also poses a theological crisis because the pastors must keep their minions happy. If the pastor's job is to comfort the afflicted and to afflict the comfortable, a balance is obviously easier to maintain with a Jewish minion than an American minion, as mentioned earlier. In other words, because of how churches are financed, the pastor today must be an expert in crowd control in a society focused more on media entertainment than biblical literacy. Maintaining faithful teaching in the midst of this framework is understandably difficult.

Change as Transition

It helpful to think of change as a transition with beginning, middle, and ending phases rather than single event. In pastoral care, the typical hospital visit is a transition—something prompted the visit, the patient requires a period of treatment, and, then, what will be different as they leave the hospital? This final question is inherently spiritual, especially when a near-death experience is involved.

The classical biblical transition is the Exodus. It took Moses maybe forty days to get the people of Israel out of Egypt, but it took forty years in the desert to get the Egypt out of the people. Even then, Joshua, not Moses, was the one who led them into the Promised Land (Bridges 2003, 43). Interestingly, it was in the desert —the middle part of the transition—where the people of Israel learned to rely on God (Exod 7:16; Card 2005).

Rebooting a Program or Career

Whenever one invests heavily in a project, program, or career, it becomes like human capital, analogous to the purchase a specialized machine, like a corn harvester (Johnson and Quance 1972). Once this investment is made, it is fixed and cannot be easily changed. When market conditions change, the value of this investment declines and may become worthless—a harvester is more profitable with six-dollar corn than two-dollar corn. Still, for the manager making the investment, it may be easier pretending markets will come back than owning up to the loss.

Early in my economics career, I invested about two years effort learning Spanish, hoping to work in Latin

American affairs. By the time I completed my degree, interest in Latin American development had subsided, and everyone was taking about West Africa development, where the dominant language in French, not Spanish. Consequently, I studied French. Before long, my career took me into finance, where my language skills were pretty much irrelevant. My willingness to learn new things and switch fields paid off—I retired with a salary about double that of colleagues who had started out with me in international affairs.

Rebooting programs and careers is an ongoing battle. The need to go to the Lord in prayer is important both in knowing what to do and in managing the painful emotions that change can bring.

Christian Distinctives

One of the most important roles Christian leaders play is distinguishing Christian beliefs from beliefs from other religions. If our spirituality is practiced theology, then right action follows primarily from right beliefs.

Let me focus on two deviations from orthodox Christian belief. First, why do Christians believe in original sin? Second, why does Christ provide the exclusive path to God's salvation?

Original Sin

Original sin describes Adam and Eve's disobedience in breaking God's command not to eat from the fruit of the tree of the knowledge of good and evil (Gen 2:17; 3:6). As a consequence, God cast them out of the Garden of Eden. Ever since, sin has tainted humanity.

Because of the doctrine of original sin, Christians are seldom surprised by sinful behavior and the existence of evil. Consequently, considerable effort has been made over time to promote moral behavior, avoiding sin and embracing godliness.

Recently, some have questioned the doctrine of sin,

arguing humanity is basically good and teaching morality is unnecessary because it only induces guilt among those taught.

An important implication of this new teaching is basically good people have no need of salvation from sin or reconciliation with God. Thus, Jesus cannot have died for our sins, need not have been divine, and was not the son of God. Thus, original sin, as taught in scripture (e.g. 1 Cor 15), is a key to understanding our need for salvation and Christ's work on the cross to bridge the gap between a holy God and unholy human beings.

The Exclusivity of Christ

Holiness is not the only gap that needs to be bridged between us and God. God creating the heavens and the earth (Gen 1:1), which means that God created time and space—attributes of the created universe. Much like carpenters are separated from the book shelves that they built, God stands outside the universe he created, an attribute known as transcendence.

God's transcendence implies we cannot approach God because God stands outside of time and space while we are locked inside both. Existentially, we cannot reach out to God; he must reach out to us. As Christians, we believe that God reached out to humanity in the person of Jesus Christ, who is both God and man—a necessary attribute to bridge the existential gap between us and God (Heb 7).

The creation account in Genesis thus eliminates the possibility the pantheists are correct in believing that God is in every living and inanimate thing because God stands apart from his creation. Also eliminated is the Jainist notion of multiple paths up the mountain to God. God's transcendence implies there are no paths up the mountain, God must come down. Christ is also not just another avatar (an incarnation of Visnu bridging the gap between God and humanity) because his sacrifice on the cross bridged the gap between God and humanity for once and for all—God need not reach out a second time.

Moving On

Orthodox Christianity grew up in the polytheistic environment of the first century, distinguished itself from many other religions, and thrived to become one and only truly world religion not linked to one language or ethnic group. Christian leaders today need to understand this history in order to witness in our interconnected world. Fear of other religions stems primarily from ignorance of the strengths of our own faith in Jesus Christ.

Show, Don't Tell

> *Let your light shine before others,*
> *so that they may see your good works and*
> *give glory to your Father who is in heaven.*
> (Matt 5:16)

*J*esus told a lot of stories.

The importance of storytelling has been long recognized among psychiatrists. Child psychologist Bruno Bettelheim (1991) saw fairy tales as playing a key role in child development because the stories offered children a template for understanding their own emotional struggles. Biblical stories serve the same function, rehearsing events from the past with current emotional, relational, and spiritual relevance.

Psychiatrist Milton Erickson was famous for his ability to reach particularly difficult psychiatric patients through hypnosis. Under hypnosis, when presumably he had more leverage to offer patients suggestion, he preferred to tell them stories of healing rather than issuing directives. These stories of healing allowed him to step around the problem of patient resistance while giving the patient a template for resolving their issues on their own (Rosen 1982).

Recognizing Stories

Savage classifies five stories to flag the emotional content in conversation during pastoral visits:

1. Reinvestment stories, where our loyalties change dramatically, such as when someone switches careers.

2. Rehearsal stories, where events from the past have current meaning, such as Bible narratives.

3. "I know someone who" stories, which mask the true storyteller.

4. Anniversary stories, which occur on an emotionally-significant calendar date, such as Christmas.

5. Transition stories, which are three-part stories, such as a trip to the hospital (why, what happened, and what comes next; Savage 1998, 95).

We cannot help but tell our stories. For years, I said the Hiemstra family was so quiet that someone could walk into the room, shoot somebody, and no one would say anything. Only recently, I realized this story captured my angst about being drafted into the Vietnam War as a young person—my draft number was thirteen, when in the prior year numbers up to one hundred, fifty-three were called. When the war ended a month before I would have been called, I felt God had graciously intervened in my life.

Parable and Explanation

Jesus' Parable of the Sower, which is found in three of the four Gospels accounts, stands out because after telling the parable he explains its meaning to the disciples, allowing Gospel readers the benefit of both left-brain and right-brain versions of the story.

Jesus' use of this parable provides a template for preaching. Hearers of the Gospel not only have different responses to the message, reflecting the different types of soil seeds can fall on, they also learn differently. Some respond to allegory and metaphor; others just want to have things explained. A sermon can accommodate each of these needs through use of prayers, personal stories, scripture readings, and didactic lessons. If the sermon's theme is also reinforced in the music, then the worship service can provide a highly integrated means of communication.

The Good Example

Bad examples litter the landscape of the postmodern

world where drug use is being de-criminalized, prostitution is being promoted as just another vocation, and shoot-them-up gaming has become a competitive sport. With our eyes on Christ, each of us as Christians should strive to be a good role model.

Much like good writers try to "show, rather than tell" their stories, good Christians act out their faith on life's stage where the lights never go out. Our role extends from birth to death. This is why we strive to improve our characters and habits with the help of the Holy Spirit.

Showing rather telling becomes particularly important in witnessing to people afflicted with pride, who refuse advice much like Erickson's psychiatric patients. Extremely intelligent and wealthy people often view themselves as too clever for everyone else, much like many teenagers. This implies that they need to learn for themselves, reflecting on the examples of others or stories told through film, theatre, conversation, or a well-chosen book.

From the Heart

Christian leadership often begins with a broken heart. In Mark's Gospel we read:

> When he went ashore he saw a great crowd, and he had compassion on them, because they were like sheep without a shepherd. And he began to teach them many things. (Mark 6:34)

How do you react to seeing friends and family trapped in needless sin and pain?

The call to action in many of my essays starts with citing statistics on suicide, often a result of despair and loss of hope. For me, suicide is personal because I lost my first best friend as a kid after his father shot himself to death and the family moved away. For Christians, suicide is needless because it indicates a lost opportunity to share the joy we have.

What moves you to act?

Heifetz and Linsky's (2002, 14, 18) distinguish technical from adaptive challenges. In a technical change, authorities apply current know-how to solve a problem while in an adaptive change people with the problem must learn new ways to solve the problem. A technical change typically requires nothing more than additional budget while an adaptive change requires an entirely new approach. Changing a program is easier than changing ourselves.

This distinction between technical and adaptive changes is helpful. Making technical changes when adaptive change is needed is the classic bureaucratic ruse to show progress in an organization sliding downhill. Grabbing for low hanging fruit is safe and permits the manager to petition for increased budget without asking for other sacrifices or convincing anyone to change how they approach their work. This is like the annual church appeal for members to bring a friend to worship as a response to declining membership.

Adaptive changes require something fundamental to change. Consider the aging white congregation located in what has now become a Hispanic or African-American neighborhood. Asking members to invite a friend to church is probably not going to stimulate a lot of new members at this church. An adaptive response might be to plan holding events for the new neighbors—something harder; something riskier. Christian leadership often requires difficult heart work before any real action can be taken.

SPECIAL ISSUES

Striving to be sensitive to the Holy Spirit, I have highlighted the issues that have recently touched my own life, including:

- Everyone is touched by grief. Christian leaders should teach others to walk alongside of the grieving rather than practicing denial to avoid repressed grief.

- Unpaid work differences between men and women leads to unwarranted differences in compensation. Recognizing the source of these differences is a first step in advocating solutions.

- The parable of the lost sheep should inform our attitude about sinners, including bad shepherds. Jesus sees people, not in terms of their sin, but in terms of who they can become.

- The healthcare consequences of sexual immorality are too large to ignore. Jesus' words to the woman caught in adultery—neither do I judge you; go and sin no more—should inform our response.

- We should all strive to finish well in this life and encourage others to do the same by taking risks to advance God's Kingdom.

- We serve a God of abundance, the sign of God's work in our lives.

Many more worthy issues could have been added to this list.

Authentic Grief

> *For godly grief produces a repentance that leads to salvation without regret, whereas worldly grief produces death.*
> (2 Cor 7:10)

About half of the patients I visited with in the emergency room during my time at Providence Hospital suffered physical maladies as a consequence of unresolved grief. Presenting diagnoses, such as backache, stroke, heart attack, head ache, suicide, addiction, obesity, and failed psychiatric intervention, often resulted from unresolved grief over the loss of a close family member. Treating the presenting diagnosis proved secondary to helping them cope with their loss.

American society does not cope with grief adequately and often encourages denial of the grieving process. Consequently, we often mask our grief with physical ailments to garner support not otherwise provided.

Godly Grief

The tension that we feel within ourselves when we

mourn forces us to decide: Do we lean into our pain or turn it over to God? Standing under the shadow of the cross at Gethsemane, Jesus had to decide whether to proceed to the cross being obedient to the will of God or to seek another future (Matt 26:42). I have often referred to this decision as a "Gethsemane moment."

Widening Our View of Grief

Our grief arises out of the loss of things that are important to us. In writing about the second Beatitude, Graham (1955, 20–26) identified five objects of mourning:

- Inadequacy—before you can grow strong, you must recognize your own weakness;

- Repentance—before you can ask for repentance, you must recognize your sin;

- Love—our compassion for the suffering of our brothers and sisters takes the form of mourning and measures our love of God;

- Soul travail—groaning for the salvation of the lost around us; and

- Bereavement—mourning over those who have passed away.

Mitchell and Anderson (1983, 36–45) widen this list to identify six major types of loss, including:

1. Material loss;
2. Relationship loss;
3. Intra-psychic loss—loss of a dream;
4. Functional loss—including loss of autonomy;
5. Role loss—like retirement; and
6. Systemic loss—like departure from your family of origin.

Each loss must be separately grieved. Elderly people find themselves experiencing many of these losses and grieving them surrounded by loved ones who may be completely unaware. But we all face losses that challenge the assumptions by which we live.

Is it any wonder that grief is the only emotion in Jesus' list of Beatitudes? (Matt 5:4)

Ministering to Those in Pain

Do you give grieving people permission to grieve or do encourage them to deny it? Van Duivendyk (2006, 3) observes:

> So many well-meaning friends and loved ones may try to cheer us up rather than just be with us in our sadness. Rather than help us grieve through and talk out our pain, they may attempt to talk us out of pain. Rather than be sojourners with us in the wilderness,

they may attempt to find us a shortcut.

Jesus openly cried over Lazarus and the widow's son, and raised them both from the dead even though no words of faith were spoken (John 11:1–46; Luke 7:11–17). This suggests that we should give permission to those in grief to mourn rather advocate a stiff upper lip, like the stoics.

Worden (2009, 39–50) divides the process of mourning into four tasks:

1. Accepting the reality of the loss,
2. Working through the pain,
3. Adjusting to a world without the deceased, and
4. Finding connection with the deceased while moving on.

The first task is to get beyond denial—a funeral with an open casket helps mourners get over the denial. The second task has to deal with the pain that may be accompanied by anxiety, anger, guilt, depression, and loneliness. The third task is to account for all the activities that the deceased shared with you and to find alternative arrangements. The fourth task is to re-evaluate your relationship with the deceased while moving on.

Unresolved grief—getting stuck in one of the tasks

above—results in anxiety attacks and physical ailments when people refuse to recognize their pain. American culture is complicit in promoting unresolved grief because co-workers, neighbors, and friends often give a grieving spouse or parent about two weeks before signaling that something is wrong if they are not over it.

It is accordingly important in funerals to give the grieving permission to grieve. This will not only help them develop a healthy grieving process, but also signal their support group that two weeks is unlikely to be a sufficient period to complete the tasks of grieving.

Unpaid Work

*E*qual pay between men and women in the workplace is impossible in the current cultural environment because they face different social expectations inside and outside the workplace. Cultural expectations of women disadvantage them in the area of unpaid, professional work that directly affects current and future salary compensation.

Christian Perspective on Equality

Although a diversity of opinion exists about how Christians should relate to each other within the family, little diversity of opinion exists about the need for Christians to live in and value family life. We are created male and female equally in the image of God (Gen 1:27), and we cannot fulfill God's command to "be fruitful and multiple" without working together (Gen 1:28). The Apostle Paul underscores this equality of the sexes when he writes about our equality in Christ (Gal 3:28).

The diversity of opinion arises from the division of labor between husband and wife stated in biblical accounts. For example, after eating from the Tree of the Knowledge of Good and Evil, God curses Eve saying: "I will surely multiply your pain in childbearing." (Gen 3:16) Meanwhile, God curses the ground to bear "thorns and thistles" increasing Adam's labor in the fields to grow food (Gen 3:18). The implication is that Eve is to be busy with the kids while Adam works the fields.

This division of labor is often viewed as prescriptive for husbands and wives today, but, even in rural settings in the developing world today, women also work the fields. Reading more closely in the Genesis account, we also see that this division of labor is not ideal—it only comes after the fall. The biblical ideal is better read as we are equal under God, and we should do what we must to be faithful servants. We must look elsewhere to explain the disparity in men and women's wages, but be sensitive to the divine intention.

Presuppositions and Discrimination

In human capital theory, economists have two working definitions of discrimination. The Civil Rights Act of 1964 made both types of discrimination illegal, but it is helpful to distinguish these types in order to come up with effective policy alternatives.

The first type of discrimination is based on

preference (Becker 1957). If I find a group disagreeable, then I will be willing to pay a penalty to avoid associating with them.

The prescription for dealing with this type of discrimination is to raise the legal penalty for disobeying the law. Thus, someone alleging discrimination has a legal right to file a lawsuit and ask for penalties to be assessed to recoup losses accrued on account of the discrimination. If wage differences continue to exist in spite of legal prohibitions, continuing wage differences are likely due to something other than preference discrimination.

The second type of discrimination is statistical discrimination (Thurow 1975). Statistical discrimination occurs when observations from past experience with members of a group are applied unreflectively to new individuals. The calculus would be something like in the past, people from group A were worth $10 a hour while those from group B were worth $15, so I will pay individual A+1 $10 and individual B+1 $15 without bothering to explore their actual education and work experience. If this behavior is reinforced by market competition, then managers paying equal wages would be at a competitive disadvantage.

The prescription for statistical discrimination is to assign the search costs to evaluate work experience to the individuals applying for work because this removes the incentive to discriminate on the basis of rules of thumb from the employer's past experience. Other prescriptions have included the use of quotas in hiring. These sorts of policies would assure that high-productivity workers do not suffer discrimination, but wage differences would continue for low-productivity workers.

Market Competition

If women's work is equal to men's work and preference discrimination is present, then companies could hire only women and drive the discriminating companies out of business on account of their misogyny. Because we seldom see this sort of behavior, wage differences are likely due to statistical, not preference, discrimination or to lower productivity.

The Nature of Work

Aspects of wage determination seriously disadvantage women, especially in skilled occupations. In skilled occupations employees constantly need to learn new things to keep up. Returning to the ideal of human capital, when an employer pays an employee a wage, part of the wage pays for today's work and part pays for future work. We would expect therefore that if women are disadvantaged in learning new skills, then we would expect them to earn less in proportion to the amount of skill required in a particular occupation.

The key disadvantage in this context arises because of unpaid, professional work. Unpaid work occurs when an employee works sixty hours a week, but is only paid for forty hours. Unpaid work is a significant portion of the work done in most salaried positions today, and it has increased with the almost ubiquitous availability of cell phones and laptop computers.

Unpaid work has two important outcomes that affect wages. Unpaid work lowers the effective wage and it increases the amount of job-related training that employees engage in. Unpaid work is sometimes required but more normally, it is at the discretion of the employee. If women as a group engage in less unpaid work than men, then wages will naturally reflect that difference.

Policy Alternative

If social obligations make it impossible for women to engage in as much unpaid work as men, then employers are aware of these differences and forcing them to pay men and women the same wage will result in fewer women being hired.

Recognizing that unpaid work is the source of the wage discrepancy suggests that employers could level the playing field by limiting opportunities to engage in unpaid work or by turning unpaid work into paid work. Penalizing unpaid work would level the playing field, but would also discourage on-the-job training, putting wage equality at odds with innovation and economic growth.

Facing an increasingly competitive global work environment, policy makers have been given difficult choices. The increasing participation of women in the workforce helped offset declining standards of living after 1980, but it also raised the opportunity cost of having children and contributed to falling fertility rates. As Americans have had fewer children, economic growth rates have been maintained through quietly encouraging immigration.

Personal Response

In our family, my wife and I had children in our thirties and my wife stayed home for ten years while our three kids were young. The kids were born about sixteen months apart to minimize her time at home. Although my wife trained as an engineer, she found that teaching mathematics and chemistry in the local high schools was more compatible with family life and she enjoyed teaching. Having her work was not so much an income-maximizing activity as an effective hedge against uncertainty in my own employment prospects.

What is the Christian response to a difficult workplace? We are called to live in families and value family life.

A Sheep Story

*M*oderation. Balance. How do we live out these admonitions in a world that paints everything in stark extremes of black and white?

Jesus tells a story:

> What man of you, having a hundred sheep, if he has lost one of them, does not leave the ninety-nine in the open country, and go after the one that is lost, until he finds it? And when he has found it, he lays it on his shoulders, rejoicing. And when he comes home, he calls together his friends and his neighbors, saying to them, rejoice with me, for I have found my sheep that was lost. Just so, I tell you, there will be more joy in heaven over one sinner who repents than over ninety-nine righteous persons who need no repentance. (Luke 15:4–7)

This story is laconic. We are not told why the sheep became lost, only that it repented. From the context, we know that the sheep is loved enough to be pursued at great cost until found. This is probably the Bible's most important lesson in dealing with sinners. God really does love you, enough to send his only son to die for you.

The Good Shepherd

Luke's story about the Good Shepherd focuses on

God's attitude about the lost, which we know because he immediately tells two other stories about something lost—a woman who lost a coin (Luke 15:8–10) and a father who almost lost his son (Luke 15:13–32). But Luke wrote like a journalist interviewing eye witnesses to the Gospel stories; he was not himself an eye witness. For an eye-witness to the context of the Good Shepherd, we must turn to John's Gospel.

Jesus declares himself to be the Good Shepherd in John 10. The context before and after the story of the good shepherd displays the tension between good and bad shepherds. Sheep recognize good shepherds. The man born blind in John 9 recognizes Jesus and comes to faith. Bad shepherds show up in John 10:19 where Jesus enters into a nasty debate with Jewish leaders.

Bad Shepherds

The timing of this debate reinforces the chapter focus on bad shepherds. The healing of the blind man occurred during the Feast of Tabernacles (or booths, John 7:1), while the shepherd discussion takes place during the Feast of Dedication (Hanukkah; John 10:22). Hanukkah commemorates the re-dedication of the temple by Judas Maccabees in 165 BC. Previously, the Maccabees led a rebellion against the Hellenization of Israel and desecration of the temple by Antiochus Epiphanies, a very bad shepherd! While we might read this chapter in light of Psalm 23 (good shepherd), John's context suggests that this story is better read in light of Ezekiel 34 (bad shepherd).

So how do we recognize a bad shepherd? We read:

> Son of man, prophesy against the shepherds of Israel; prophesy, and say to them, even to the shepherds, Thus says the Lord GOD: Ah, shepherds of Israel who have been feeding yourselves! Should not shepherds feed the sheep? (Ezekiel 34:2)

In Jesus' context, the bad shepherds in view were the Sadducees, who controlled access to the temple and the sacrifices being offered, and the Pharisees, who were jealous of Jesus. More generally, the bad shepherds are those "feeding themselves," earning a paycheck while avoiding unpopular teaching and unpopular people, like the poor and outcasts.

The Ethical Problem

An ethical problem arises when two theological principles come into conflict. On the one hand, we are instructed "Go therefore and make disciples of all nations."

(Matt 28:19) Yet, we are also told:

> Not to associate with anyone who bears the name of brother or sister if he is guilty of sexual immorality or greed, or is an idolater, reviler, drunkard, or swindler—not even to eat with such a one. (1 Cor 5:11)

Setting aside the finesse of who is and is not a disciple and when, these two admonitions are obviously in conflict.

In this context, the words of Jesus in John 8 are appropriate. In addressing the woman caught in adultery, Jesus says:

> Woman, where are they? Has no one condemned you? She said, no one, Lord. And Jesus said, neither do I condemn you; go, and from now on sin no more. (John 8:10–11)

For many people, Jesus' words to the woman caught in adultery are a hard teaching—some because Jesus let the woman off easy; others because he required her to relinquish her sin. When the Bible bothers us, our role as Christian leaders is not to dismiss it, but rather to find creative ways to honor it and bring glory to God.

Misplaced Affections

The radio silence today on discussions of morality is killing people.

In my annual physical this year, my doctor indicated that the U.S. Center for Disease Control and Prevention (CDC) now recommends that all Baby Boomers be screened for hepatitis C:

> There is increasing HCV [hepatitis C virus]-associated morbidity and mortality, as annual HCV-associated mortality in the US increased more than 50% from 1999 to 2007 [currently 3.5 million cases]. People born 1945–1965 with hepatitis C face increasing hepatitis C-associated morbidity and mortality. (CDC 2019b)

What is stunning is how hepatitis is usually contracted:

> Although transmission via injection drug use remains the most common mode of HCV acquisition in the United States, sexual transmission is an important mode of acquisition among HIV-infected MSM [men having sex with men] with risk factors, including those who participate in unprotected anal intercourse, use sex toys, and use non-injection drugs. (CDC 2019a)

While one might contract hepatitis in a third-world country through exposure to unprotected water, in the

United States one generally needs to engage in high-risk behavior to contract the disease.

Public Health Crises

High-risk behavior has become a public health hazard in the United States. Given our recent experience with Acquired Immuno-Deficiency Syndrome (AIDS), this conclusion should come as no surprise.

Roughly 675,000 people have died in the United States from AIDS, according to the CDC (2016). In addition, there were 1.1 million people in the United States infected with AIDS in 2015. Two-thirds of them were gay men. Most of the rest have been intravenous drug users, although spouses of victims can also contract the disease. The average lifetime treatment cost in 2010 dollars was $379,668, which implies a drug market of roughly half a trillion dollars, one of the nation's largest (CDC 2017, 2018a).

On top of HCV and human immunodeficiency virus (HIV) infection, the number of sexually transmitted diseases (STDs—chlamydia, gonorrhea, syphilis, and chancroid) have growing rapidly over the past decade, especially among millennials and the elderly. A thirty-one percent increase between 2012 and 2017 (2.3 million cases) in reported STDs cases reversed a decline in reported cases that began in the 1940s (CDC 2018b). Today's sexual liberality bears much of the blame for these outcomes.

Taking Stock

Perhaps you are thinking, why do I care? Isn't using a condom sufficient caution and isn't there a pill for every one of these diseases? The answer today is a qualified yes. Yes—if you are diagnosed early, then these diseases are treatable. There may even soon be a cure for AIDS.

The trouble is that not everyone is prudent in their relationships, has a healthcare plan, and gets a prompt diagnosis. Sex is often exchanged for drugs, and it has an addictive quality that often leads to taking more risks. More troubling is the observation that diseases often mutate into new, more viral strains—twenty years ago no one had heard of HCV and before 1980 no one had heard of HIV.

For those that want to limit this conversation to the realm of personal freedom and conversations with their doctors, the opioid crisis raises the specter of conflicting incentives in the healthcare system. More than 200,000

Americans have died from opioid overdoses. Many of these addictions began with prescription painkillers known to be addictive and very profitable for the companies producing them (e.g. WP 2019).

Treating AIDS is expensive and it may also be more profitable than treating other illnesses. What happens if drug companies and other healthcare providers become complicit in promoting alternative lifestyles motivated by their economic interest rather than care for those afflicted? This is not a moot point: Among the 379 companies filling an amicus brief before the Supreme Court on *Obergefell v. Hodges* were some of the largest drug companies in the United States. (Wener-Fligner 2015)

Who exactly can you trust when so much money is changing hands?

Toward a Christian Perspective

Before any conversation about moral behavior, know that God loves you because he created you and sent his son, Jesus Christ, to die for you. God's love is extended unconditionally, irrespective of your healthcare status. But God's love is a gift that must be accepted. The consequences of rejecting God's love (or holding it lightly) can be severe.

The teaching of the church on the question of human sexuality has been clear since biblical times (Fortson and Grams 2016). Sex is reserved for married couples in a lifelong relationship between one man and one woman. All other sexual activity is sin, which Christians are advised to avoid (Gagnon 2001).

The focus of a disciplined life is on God. Extramarital sex leads to other priorities and denigrates the image of God that we should look for in other people. One pastor I know makes the point that he always knows when kids start having sex because they soon drop out of church.

Doing Better

Knowing that the healthcare consequences of sexual immorality can be severe, the critical question for those wavering on their response is: If by your words or actions, you lead someone into risky behavior, are you okay with the pain and other consequences they suffer? Are you okay, for example, with rising healthcare costs mean that more young mothers cannot afford care for their kids while the nation's healthcare budget is diverted into other priorities?

One of the most tortured women that I ever met was an HIV-positive prostitute who lost custody of her kids back in 2011. At one point, she considered herself a consenting adult. Now, her kids have lost their mother. We cannot anticipate all the consequences of our decisions—the best we can do is to rely on God's help to make better decisions.

Mary Eberstadt cites four prophecies appear to have taken place because of the greater use of contraceptives since the 1960s:

> A general lowering of moral standards throughout society; a rise in infidelity; a lessening of respect for women by men; and the coercive use of reproductive technologies by governments. (Pope Paul VI 2014, 11)

If it is too late for you to worry about the above moral issues, remember that we worship a God of second chances. Turn to him and find forgiveness.

Covered and Healed

> *For we know,*
> *brothers and sisters loved by God,*
> *that he has chosen you,*
> *because our gospel came to you*
> *not only in word, but also in power and*
> *in the Holy Spirit and with full conviction.*
> (1 Thes 1:4–5)

Do you truly feel forgiven and loved by God?

It is one thing to know conceptually that you are covered by the blood of Jesus and it is another thing to feel it in your heart.

Fear and Anxiety

In 2010, I signed up for a small group discussion at church. The pastor's wife later called to ask whether I would be willing to switch to another group that was studying fear.

No problem, I said.

But, thinking to myself—Why would I want to join a group talking about fear?

Later, as I read Max Lucado's *Fearless*, I realized that

I had a deep-seated fear of not mattering, of disappointing God, and of not being able to protect my wife and kids from a long list off worst-case scenarios in a drifting culture (Lucado 2009, ix). Not only had fear crept into my life, it was dictating a lot of my decisions. Through almost no effort on my part, God had directed me to a major stronghold in my life and helped me deal with it.

Max Lucado (2009, 5–6) observed that ordinary children today are more fearful than psychiatric patients were in the 1950s. Fear displaces happiness; fear is unproductive; fear is self-defeating. Fear of losing one's children, one's job, or one's health can paralyze a person. Who can contemplate Einstein's theory of relativity when one worries about the roof collapsing?

In the midst of their fears after the storm on the Sea of Galilee, Jesus asked his disciples: Why were you afraid? (Matthew 8:26)

Emergency Department

In 2019, I made a trip to Cambridge, Massachusetts to visit my daughter and her husband. We had a wonderful time together, but two days before my return home, I ate something that set off my stomach and it exacerbated a problem with my prostrate. Unable to urinate, I ended up in the local hospital in the emergency department where they inserted a catheter, which I lived with for about two weeks. Although movement of almost any kind was uncomfortable, I was able to travel home but I was unable to pursue my normal activities—writing, exercising, volunteering, church attendance—during my convalescence.

Embarrassed by my condition, I did not advertise my sudden dependency on the good graces of my friends and family. Nevertheless, word got around and I soon found three churches and a lot of friends praying over me. Meanwhile, my wife proved herself to be an absolute angel.

A great peace came over me. For the first time in recent memory, I found myself anxiety-free. I have always felt God's love; now, I felt loved like never before by my family and the church. Being a lifelong nervous eater, this peace displaced interest in food and I lost more than ten pounds, a healing brought about by this peace.

Loved by God

We serve a God of abundance. The Apostle John

recognized the divinity of Christ through his miracles of abundance: Wine, loaves of bread, and fish (John 2, 6, 21). The trademark of God's healing displays itself as healing that extends beyond the presenting diagnosis. In my case, I no longer need a catheter and I continue to enjoy a deep peace.

CONCLUSION

Wrapping Up

In my journey to understand the depth of Christian spirituality I frequently cite four questions taken from philosophy:

1. Metaphysics—who is God?
2. Anthropology—who are we?
3. Epistemology—how do we know?
4. Ethics—what do we do about it? (Kreeft 2007, 6)

As an author, my first two books—*A Christian Guide to Spirituality* and *Life in Tension*—address the metaphysical question and my third book—*Called Along the Way*—explores the anthropological question in the first person. My fourth book, *Simple Faith*, examined the epistemological question. In *Living in Christ*, I have focused on ethics, the fourth question. Serious problems arise when one of these questions is neglected.

Neglect of Metaphysics

Postmodern culture's almost exclusive focus on the physical world neglects the metaphysical. Metaphysics literally means above physics or, better, beyond physics.

Postmodern people struggle to understand God, especially his transcendence.

Having created the known universe, God stands apart from it or, in other words, he transcends the universe. For us as mortal human beings, no path takes us up the mountain to God, God must come down to us. As Christians, we believe that he came to us in the person of Jesus Christ.

Neglect of metaphysics shows up in the popular expression: I am spiritual, just not religious. Here spirituality is defined as limited to the human experience, especial feelings of ecstasy—great joy or happiness, even if drug induced. Postmodern people seem stuck in a moment of time believing that the physical world is all that there is. Soon, life seems pointless—especially when circumstance take a nasty turn, as with the corona virus pandemic.

Neglect of Anthropology

The neglect of anthropology manifests itself in the acceptance of Greek anthropology where heart and mind are separate. Emotions are more valued or thinking is more valued, depending on who you talk to, but the two are held to be distinctly different. This separation poses a problem for faith because faith requires heart and mind to be considered together.

While this subject is timely, it is not new. Theologian Jonathan Edwards (2009, 13), writing in 1746 about the effects of the Great Awakening, noted that both head and heart were necessarily involved in effective discipling. He coined the phrase *holy affections* to distinguish the marks of the work of the Spirit from other works and associated these holy affections directly with scripture.

More recently, Elliott (2009, 46–47) distinguishes two theories of emotions: The cognitive theory and the non-cognitive theory. The cognitive theory of emotions argues that reason and emotion are interdependent while the non-cognitive theories promote the separation of reason and emotion. In other words, the cognitive theory states that we get emotional about the things that we strongly believe.

Elliott notes that the God of the Bible only gets angry on rare occasions when people have disobeyed the covenant or expressed a hardness of the heart, as with Pharaoh (Exod 4:21). Our emotions are neither random nor unexplained because they are not mere physiology, but rather extensions of our beliefs. Elliott (2009, 53–54) writes: "If the cognitive theory is correct, emotions become an integral part of our reason and our ethics" informing and reinforcing moral behavior.

Neglect of anthropology is perhaps the single, most important reason that the Christian faith has been hard to understand and accept in our time. If faith is viewed only through the mind, then it becomes dry and lifeless; if faith is viewed only through the emotions, then the buzz quickly wears off. Either way, a lopsided faith is soon unable to cope with life's many challenges.

Neglect of Epistemology

The neglect of epistemology is closely related to the neglect of anthropology. Few people come to faith because of intellectual arguments (epistemology is the study of knowledge), but many people who have come to faith for emotional reasons later fall away because their faith appears to lack substance. When heart and mind are not engaged together, the absence of one affects the durability of the other.

The anti-intellectualism of American culture is the great enigma of the postmodern age. The advances of technology have led to the convenience of communication and the extension of life through new medical discoveries, yet the thought processes required to develop and sustain these technologies are known to a tiny number of people. Instead, youth culture, which focuses on moral laxity, appears parasitic relative to this great intellectual heritage.

Neglect of epistemology leaves people apprehensive of the faith they have seen in others and makes it hard for them to understand the logic of faith and to accept the lifestyle changes required to join the Christian community.

Neglect of Ethics

The neglect of ethics is the problem that theological principles are in tension with one another and, rather than deal with the tension, one picks a favorite theological principle to highlight to the exclusion of others. This practice underscores the shallowness of our faith. Neglect of ethics becomes obvious in the life of the church and community more widely when political views replace honest discernment and the focus on God melts away amidst senseless conflict.

A special form of this neglect of ethics arises when people start to see the church as a "holy huddle," a kind of shelter from the storms of life, rather than as a team meeting of the faithful, searching together for answers in the midst of the struggles of life. Hollinger (2005, 16) writes: "Taken alone, thought, passion, and action render a fragmented faith that only further engenders a fragmented self and a fragmented church." Fragmented in this way, the hard tradeoffs required by limited time, energy, and resources are overlooked and growth in discipleship remains frozen in time.

Life in Tension

Considering all four of the questions taken from philosophy does not lead to a trouble-free Christian life, but it prevents the neglect of important aspects of our faith. Tension always exists between the life of the Christian and the culture we find ourselves in. We need to accept this tension and learn to live with it because without tension our lives cannot be transformed into the image of Christ and we cannot be a witness to that truth.

Summary

Our journey in Christian ethics starts with God in whose image we are created. Creation begins with birth and continues as we mature. Our character matures, shaped by the example of Christ under the mentorship of the Holy Spirit through the family and the church. Christian leaders reach full maturity once they able to mentor others —we are blessed to be a blessing.

In Galatians 3:24, the Apostle Paul describes Old Testament law as a guardian of righteousness. Ethics is often equated with law, but law only provides the most general boundaries to our actions. Who we are, our influences, and our aspirations subtly shape our actions, often without our conscious awareness. This subtly links our character to our community and molds the kind of leaders that we become. It also makes it difficult to define ethics outside the bounds of a particular community, like the faith community.

The Bible takes words seriously, yet the God of the Bible does not prefer any particular human language. The church could be defined as a community where people listen to one another and to God. Listening is important because ethics requires interpretation of the Bible and of events under the guidance of the Holy Spirit. Worshiping God and maintaining a listening ear requires the Sabbath be taken seriously. Being the church requires sheltering the entire community, especially widows, orphans, and immigrants, during hard times.

Christian leadership extends our Christian character as we mentor others and it is the most important application of our faith. Our capacity to assume this mentorship role depends on how we care for our own souls. Our pursuit of holiness and our practice of godliness serve in developing our character and making others aware of it.

Part of this practice is caring for those in our own families, especially the young and the elderly. Part of this practice is understanding the context and presuppositions supporting good character. Part of this is being able to assist others in managing difficult transitions in life. Part of this is being a good example that Christ calls us to be. It starts as we manifest the heart of Christ.

Striving to be sensitive to the Holy Spirit, I highlight the issues that have recently touched my own life, including:

- Everyone is touched by grief. Christian leaders should teach others to walk alongside of the grieving rather than practicing denial.

- Unpaid work differences between men and women leads to unwarranted differences in compensation. Recognizing the source of these differences is a first step in advocating solutions.

- The parable of the lost sheep should inform our attitude about sinners. Jesus sees people, not in terms of their sin, but in terms of who they can become.

- The healthcare consequences of sexual immorality are too large to ignore.

- We should all strive to finish well and encourage others to do the same.

- We serve a God of abundance.

Hopefully, discussing my own challenges has also blessed you.

Finding Closure

> *Jesus said to him,*
> *No one who puts his hand to the plow and*
> *looks back is fit for the kingdom of God.*
> (Luke 9:62)

*I*t's not how you start, but how you finish that matters to the Lord.

Remember Jesus's words to the woman caught in adultery:

> Jesus stood up and said to her, Woman, where are they? Has no one condemned you? She said, No one, Lord. And Jesus said, neither do I condemn you; go, and from now on sin no more. (John 8:10–11)

We all have history. In Jesus Christ we share the opportunity to live into a future defined by who God says we are, not by our own sins. This is our freedom in Christ.

The Plow

The reference to the plow in Luke 9:62 (cited above) recalls the calling of Elisha the prophet:

> So he departed from there and found Elisha the son of Shaphat, who was plowing with twelve yoke of oxen in front of him, and he was with the twelfth. Elijah passed by him

and cast his cloak upon him. And he left the oxen and ran after Elijah and said, let me kiss my father and my mother, and then I will follow you. And he said to him, go back again, for what have I done to you? And he returned from following him and took the yoke of oxen and sacrificed them and boiled their flesh with the yokes of the oxen and gave it to the people, and they ate. Then he arose and went after Elijah and assisted him. (1 Kgs 19:19–21)

No one questions the commitment of Elisha to follow Elijah, but Jesus' ministry demands a higher level of commitment.

Os Guinness recounts the story of eighteen-year-old Jane Lucretia D'Esterre, his own great-great-grandmother, who, distraught over the death of her husband in an 1815 duel, went to a river to drown herself. There she noticed the son of a neighbor plowing a field:

> Meticulous, absorbed, skilled, he displayed such as pride in his work that the newly turned furrows looked as finely executed as the paint strokes on an artist's canvas. (Guinness 2003, 184)

Seeing this young man work, she gave up thoughts of suicide.

Guinness' story highlights the importance of attending to our daily work as service not only for our supervisors but for the Lord. Suppose someone contemplating suicide watched you work. Would they find courage to face life again?

Finishing Well

The need to take risks to advance God's kingdom is highlighted in Jesus' Parable of the Talents. Here, Jesus describes a businessman who, in preparing for a trip, leaves his assets in the hands of trusted assistants. The first receiving, for example, a million dollars, another two million, and a third five million.

When he returned from his trip, he asked for an accounting from his assistants. The latter two assistants invested his money and doubled it, earning their bosses' praise: Well done, good and faithful servants. The businessman then promoted these assistants.

By contrast, the first assistant stashed the boss' money in a vault and simple returned what he had been given. Seeing no gain from his confidence in this first assistant, the businessman called him lazy and gave his million to the assistant now holding ten. The businessman then fired this assistant and sent him away (Matt 25: 14–30).

Celebrate the Season

I have always sensed urgency in my work. Rather than running from one task to another, however, I have learned to celebrate the seasons of life by completing them and marking their completion.

Remember the people of Israel during the Exodus. Once they crossed the Red Sea and witnessed the destruction of the Egyptian army, they danced and sang praises to God: "I will sing to the Lord, for he has triumphed gloriously; the horse and his rider he has thrown into the sea." (Exod 15:1)

Later when God parted the Jordan River and they crossed into the Promised Land God instructed Joshua to mark the occasion:

> And Joshua said to them, pass on before the ark of the Lord your God into the midst of the Jordan, and take up each of you a stone upon his shoulder, according to the number of the tribes of the people of Israel, that this may be a sign among you. When your children ask in time to come, what do those stones mean to you? then you shall tell them that the waters of the Jordan were cut off before the ark of the covenant of the Lord. When it passed over the Jordan, the waters of the Jordan were cut off. So these stones shall be to the people of Israel a memorial

forever. (Josh 4:5–7)

These memory stones are called Ebenezers. Modern Ebenezers include things like birthdays, weddings, anniversaries, graduations, funerals, and lists of answered prayers.

When I have a bad day—get stuck in a moment—and need a good talking to, I often read my own prayer book. Our future in Christ, which gives my life meaning and a sense of whose I am.

REFERENCES

Bainton, Roland H. 1995. *Here I Stand: The Life of Martin Luther.* New York: Meridan.

Barth, Karl. 1959. *A Shorter Commentary on Romans* (1940). Richmond: John Knox Press.

BDAG - *Greek-English Lexicon of the New Testament and Other Early Christian Literature.* 2000. The University of Chicago Press (electronic edition). Revised and edited by Frederick William Danker based on the Walter Bauer's Griechisch-deutsches Wörterbuch zu den Schriften des Neuen Testaments und für frühchristlichen Literatur, sixth edition, ed. Kurt Aland and Barbara Aland, with Viktor Reichmann and on previous English Editions by W.F.Arndt, F.W.Gingrich, and F.W.Danker.

Becker, Gary S. 1957. *The Economics of Discrimination.* Chicago: University of Chicago Press.

Bell, James Scott 2014. *How to Write Dazzling Dialogue: The Fastest Way to Improve Any Manuscript*. Woodland Hills, CA: Compendium Press.

Benner, David G. 1998. *Care of Souls: Revisioning Christian Nurture and Counsel*. Grand Rapids: Baker Books.

Bernstein, Lenny. 2018. "U.S. life expectancy declines again, a dismal trend not seen since World War I." *Washington Post*. November 29.

Bettelheim, Bruno. 1991. *The Uses of Enchantment: The Meaning and Importance of Fairy Tales* (Orig Pub 1975). New York: Penguin Books.

BibleWorks. Norfolk: *BibleWorks*, LLC, 2011. <BibleWorks v.9>.

Blamires, Harry. 2005. *The Christian Mind: How Should a Christian Think?* (Orig Pub 1963). Vancouver: Regent College Publishing.

Bonhoeffer, Dietrich. 1954. *Life Together: The Classic Exploration of Christian Community* (Gemeinsames Leben). Translated by John W. Doberstein. New York: HarperOne.

Bonhoeffer, Dietrich. 1976. *Ethics* (Orig pub 1955). Edited by Eberhard Bethge. Translated by Neville Horton Smith. New York: MacMillan Publishers Company, Inc.

Bonhoeffer, Dietrich. 1995. *The Cost of Discipleship* (Orig Pub 1937). Translated by R. H. Fuller and Irmgard Booth. New York: Simon & Schuster—A Touchstone Book.

Boorstin, Daniel J. 1962. *The Image; or, What Happened to the American Dream*. New York: Atheneum.

Bridge, William. 2003. *Managing Transitions: Making the Most of Change*. Cambridge: Da Capo Press.

Bridges, Jerry. 1996a. *The Pursuit of Holiness*. Colorado Springs: NavPress.

Bridges, Jerry. 1996b. *The Practice of Godliness*. Colorado Springs: NavPress.

Brueggemann, Walter. 2014. *Sabbath as Resistance: Saying NO to the Culture of Now*. Louisville: Westminster John Knox Press.

Calvin, John. 1939. *A Compendium of the Institutes of the Christian Religion*. Edited by Hugh Thomson Kerr, Jr. Philadelphia: Presbyterian Board of Christian Education.

Campbell, W. P. 2010. *Turning Controversy into Church Ministry: A Christlike Response to Homosexuality*. Grand Rapids: Zondervan.

Card, Michael. 2005. *A Sacred Sorrow: Reaching Out to God in the Lost Language of Lament*. [Also: Experience Guide]. Colorado Springs: NavPress.

Center for Behavioral Health Statistics and Quality (CBHSQ). 2015. *Behavioral Health Trends in the United States: Results from the 2014 National Survey on Drug Use and Health* (Health and Human Services (HHS) Publication No. SMA 15-4927, NSDUH Series H-50). Retrieved from http://www.samhsa.gov/data. (Accessed: 18 October 2018).

Center for Disease Control (CDC). 2016. "Today's HIV/AIDS Epidemic." *CDC Factsheet*. Online: https://www.cdc.gov/nchhstp/newsroom/docs/factsheets/todaysepidemic-508.pdf. Accessed: 8 January 2019.

Center for Disease Control (CDC). 2017. *HIV Cost-effectiveness*. Online: https://www.cdc.gov/hiv/programresources/guidance/costeffectiveness/index.html. Accessed: 8 January 2019.

Center for Disease Control (CDC). 2018a. *Basic Statistics* [on AIDS]. Online: https://www.cdc.gov/hiv/basics/statistics.html. Accessed: 8 January 2019.

Center for Disease Control (CDC). 2018b. *Sexually Transmitted Disease Surveillance 2017*. Online: https://www.cdc.gov/std/stats17/2017-STD-Surveillance-Report_CDCclearance-9.10.18.pdf. Accessed: 24 September 2019.

Center for Disease Control and Prevention (CDC). 2019a. *Epidemiology and Prevention of HIV and Viral Hepatitis Co-infections*. Online: https://www.cdc.gov/hepatitis/populations/hiv.htm. Accessed: 24 September 2019.

Center for Disease Control and Prevention (CDC). 2019b. *CDC Recommendation: Adults Born from 1945–1965 (Baby Boomers) get Tested for Hepatitis C*. Online: https://www.cdc.gov/hepatitis/populations/1945-1965.htm. Accessed: 24 September 2019.

Cloud, Henry. 2008. *The One-Life Solution: Reclaiming Your Personal Life While Achieving Greater Professional Success*. New York: HarperCollins.

Cloud, Henry and John Townsend. 1992. *Boundaries: When to Say YES; When to Say NO; To Take Control of Your Life*. Grand Rapids: Zondervan.

Cross, John G. and Melvin J. Guyer. 1980. *Social Traps*. Ann Arbor: University of Michigan Press.

Crowley, Chris and Henry S. Lodge. 2007. *Younger Next Year: Live Strong, Fit, and Sexy — Until You're 80 and Beyond*. Male and Female editions. New York: Workman Publishing.

Dawn, Marva J. 1999. *A Royal "Waste" of Time: The Splendor of Worshipping God and Being Church for the World*. Grand Rapids: Eerdmans.

Dayton, Donald W. 2005. Discovering an Evangelical Heritage (Orig Pub 1976). Peabody: Hendrickson Publishers.

Defoe, Daniel. 1719. *The Life and Strange Surprising Adventures of Robinson Crusoe.* United Kingdom: William Taylor.

Derrida, Jacques. 1978. *Writing and Difference.* Translated by Alan Bass. Chicago: University of Chicago Press.

Desilver, Drew. 2018. "For most U.S. workers, real wages have barely budged in decades" Pew Research Center. Accessed: 25 July 2019. Online: (https://www.pewresearch.org/staff/drew-desilver) August 7.

Dewey, John. 1997. *How We Think* (Orig Pub 1910). Mineola, NY: Dover Publications.

Duke University. 1999. "Religious Attendance Linked to Lower Mortality in Elderly." Updated: January 20, 2016. Online: https://corporate.dukehealth.org/news-listing/religious-attendance-linked-lower-mortality-elderly Accessed: 18 January 2019.

Edwards, Jonathan. 2009. *The Religious Affections* (Orig Pub 1746). Vancouver: Eremitical Press.

Elliott, Matthew A. 2006. *Faithful Feelings: Rethinking Emotion in the New Testament.* Grand Rapids: Kregel Academic and Professional.

Fea, John. 2011. *Was America Founded as a Christian Nation? A Historical Introduction.* Louisville: Westminister John Knox Press, 2011.

Fortson, S. Donald and Rollin G. Grams. 2016. *Unchanging Witness: The Consistent Christian Teaching on Homosexuality in Scripture and Tradition.* Nashville: B&H Academic.

France, R.T. 2007. *The Gospel of Matthew. New International Commentary on the New Testament*. Grand Rapids: Eerdmans.

Friedman, Edwin H. 1985. *Generation to Generation: Family Process in Church and Synagogue*. New York: Gilford Press.

Fukuyama, Francis. 2018. *Identity: The Demand for Dignity and the Politics of Resentment*. New York: Macmillan.

Gagnon, Robert A. J. 2001. *The Bible and Homosexual Practice: Texts and Hermeneutics*. Nashville: Abingdon Press.

Galbraith, John Kenneth. 1993. *American Capitalism: The Concept of Countervailing Power* (1980). Transaction Publishers.

Gehrz, Christopher and Mark Pattie III. 2017. *The Pietist Option: Hope for the Renewal of Christianity*. Downers Grove: IVP Academic.

Giglio, Louis. 2003. *The Air I Breathe.* Colorado Springs: Multnomah Publishers.

Gilbert, Roberta M. 2006. *The Eight Concepts of Bowen Theory: A New Way of Thinking about the Individual and the Group.* Front Royal, VA: Leading Systems Press.

Goldberg, Jonah. 2009. *Liberal Fascism: The Secret History of the American Left, from Mussolini to the Politics of Change.* New York: Broadway Books.

Graham, Billy. 1955. *The Secret of Happiness.* Garden City, NY: Doubleday and Company, Inc.

Graham, Billy. 1997. *Just As I Am: An Autobiography of Billy Graham.* New York: Zondervan.

Greene, William H. 1997. *Econometric Analysis.* New Jersey: Prentice Hall.

Guinness, Os. 2003. *The Call: Finding and Fulfilling the Central Purpose of Your Life.* Nashville: Thomas Nelson.

Guinness, Os. 2013. *The Global Public Square: Religious Freedom and the Making of the World Safe for Diversity.* Downers Grove: IVP Press.

Hayasaki, Erika. 2016. "Traces of Times Lost: How childhood memories shape us, even after we've forgotten them." *The Atlantic.* November 29.

Heifetz, Ronald A. and Marty Linsky. 2002. *Leadership on the Line: Staying Alive through the Dangers of Leading.* Boston: Harvard Business School Press.

Hellerman, Joseph H. 2001. *The Ancient Church as Family.* Minneapolis: Fortress Press.

Hiemstra, Stephen W. 2009. "Can Bad Culture Kill a Firm?" pp 51–54 of *Risk Management.* Society of Actuaries. Issue 16. June.

Hiemstra, Stephen W. 2017. *Called Along the Way: A Spiritual Memoir.* Centreville, VA: T2Pneuma Publishers LLC.

Hiemstra, Stephen W. 2019. *Simple Faith: Something Worth Living For.* Centreville, VA: T2Pneuma Publishers LLC.

Hoekema, Anthony A. 1994. *Created in God's Image.* Grand Rapids: Eerdmans.

HOLL - *A Concise Hebrew and Aramaic Lexicon of the Old Testament.* 1997. Based upon the Lexical Work of Ludwig Koehler and Walter Baumgartner, edited by W.L. Holladay. Brill Academic Publishers.

Hollinger, Dennis P. 2005. *Head, Heart, and Hands: Bringing Together Christian Thought, Passion, and Action.* Downers Grove: IVP Books.

Holt, Bradley P. 2017. *Thirsty for God: A Brief History of Christian Spirituality.* Minneapolis: Fortress Press.

Johnson, Glenn L. 1986. *Research Methodology for Economists: Philosophy and Practice.* New York: MacMillan Publishing Company.

Johnson, Glenn L. and C. Leroy Quance [editors]. 1972. *The Overproduction Trap in U.S. Agriculture: A Study of Resource Allocation from World War I to the Late 1960's.* Baltimore: Johns Hopkins University Press.

Johnson, Glenn L. And Lewis K. Zerby. 1973. *What Economists Do About Values: Case Studies of Their Answers to Questions They Don't Dare Ask.* East Lansing: Michigan State University.

Jung, Carl G. 1955. *Modern Man in Search of a Soul* (Orig Pub 1933). Translated by W.S. Dell and Cary F. Baynes. New York: Harcourt, Inc.

Keener, Craig S. 2003. *The Gospel of John: A Commentary, Volume One.* Peabody: Henderickson.

Keller, Timothy and Kathy Keller. 2011. *The Meaning of Marriage: Facing the Complexities of Commitment with the Wisdom of God.* New York: Dutton.

Kreeft, Peter. 2007. *The Philosophy of Jesus*. South Bend, IN: Saint Augustine Press.

Lucado, Max. 2009. *Fearless: Imagine Your Life Without Fear*. Nashville: Thomas Nelson.

Lester, Andrew D. 2007. *Anger: Discovering Your Spiritual Ally*. Louisville: Westminster John Knox Press.

Mahan, Jeffrey H., Barbara B. Troxell, and Carol J. Allen (MTA). 1993. *Shared Wisdom: A Guide to Case Study Reflection in Ministry*. Nashville: Abingdon Press.

Mason, Karen. 2014. *Preventing Suicide: A Handbook for Pastors, Chaplains, and Pastoral Counselors*. Downers Grove: IVP Books.

May, Gerald G. 1988. *Addiction & Grace: Love and Spirituality in the Healing of Addictions*. New York: HarperOne.

McDonald, Suzanne. 2010. *Re-Imaging Election: Divine Election as Representing God to Others & Others to God*. Grand Rapids: Eerdmans.

Meadows, Donella, H. Dennis L. Meadows, Jorgen Randers, and William W. Behrens III (MMRB). 1975. *The Limits to Growth: A Report for the Club of Rome's Project on the Predicament of Mankind*. New York: Universe Books Publishers.

Metaxis, Eric. 2010. *Bonhoeffer: Pastor, Martyr, Prophet, Spy*. Nashville: Thomas Nelson.

Miller, William R. and Stephen Rollnick. 2002. *Motivational Interviews: Preparing People for Change*. New York: Guilford Press.

Mitchell, Kenneth R. and Herbert Anderson. 1983. *All Our Losses; All Our Griefs: Resources for Pastoral Care*. Louisville: Westminster John Knox Press.

Moots, Paul. 2014. *Becoming Barnabas: The Ministry of Encouragement*. Herndon: Alban Institute.

Niebuhr, H. Richard. 1937. *The Kingdom of God in America*. New York: Harper Torchbooks.

Nouwen, Henri J.M. 2002. *In the Name of Jesus: Reflections on Christian Leadership*. New York: Crossroad Publishing Company.

Patterson, Kerry Joseph Grenny, Ron McMillan, and Al Switzler (PGMS). 2012. *Crucial Conversations: Tools for Talking When Stakes Are High*. New York: McGraw-Hill.

Peterson, Eugene H. 2011. The Pastor: A Memoir. New York: Harper Collins Publishers.

Plueddemann, James E. 2009. *Leading Across Cultures: Effective Ministry and Mission in the Global Church*. Downers Grove: IVP Academic.

Pope Paul VI. 2014. *On Human Life* (Humanae Vitae). San Francisco: Ignatius Press.

Porter, Michael E. 1980. *Competitive Strategy: Techniques for Analyzing Industries and Competitors*. New York: Free Press.

Presbyterian Church in the United States of America (PCUSA). 1999. *The Constitution of the Presbyterian Church (U.S.A.) — Part I: Book of Confessions*. Louisville, KY: Office of the General Assembly.

Presbyterian Church in the United States of America (PCUSA). 2007. *The Constitution of the Presbyterian Church (USA): Part II: Book of Order 2011/2013*. Louisville, KY: Office of the General Assembly.

Presbyterian Church in the United States of America (PCUSA). 2011. *The Constitution of the Presbyterian Church (USA): Part II: Book of Order 2011/2013*. Louisville, KY: Office of the General Assembly.

Robinson, Marilynne. 2004. *Gilead: A Novel*. New York: Picador.

Rosen, Sidney. 1982. *My Voice Will Go with You: The Teaching Tales of Milton H. Erickson*. New York: W.W. Norton.

Savage, John. 1996. *Listening & Caring Skills: A Guide for Groups and Leaders*. Nashville: Abingdon Press.

Shafer-Landau, Russ. 2018. *The Fundamentals of Ethics*. New York: Oxford University Press.

Simon, Herbert A. 1997. *Administrative Behavior: A Study of Decision-Making Processes in Administrative Organizations* (Orig pub 1945). New York: Free Press.

Smith, Houston. 2001. *Why Religion Matters: The Fate of the Human Spirit in an Age of Disbelief*. San Francisco: Harper.

Smith, James K. A. 2016. *You Are What You Love: The Spiritual Power of Habit*. Grand Rapids: Brazos Press.

Smylie, James H. *A Brief History of the Presbyterians*. Louisville: Geneva Press, 1996.

Spangler, Ann, and Lois Tverberg. 2009. *Sitting at the Feet of Rabbi Jesus: How the Jewishness of Jesus Can Transform Your Faith*. Grand Rapids: Zondervan.

Stanton, Thomas H. 2012. *Why Some Firms Thrive While Others Fail: Governance and Management Lessons from the Crisis*. New York: Oxford University Press.

Stinnett, Nick and Nancy Stinnett, Joe Beam, and Alice Beam (Stinnett and Beam). 1999. *Fantastic Families: 6 Proven Steps to Building a Strong Family*. New York: Howard Books.

Tavernise, Sabrina. 2016. "U.S. Suicide Rate Surges to a 30-Year High." *New York Times*. April 22. Online: https://nyti.ms/2k9vzFZ, Accessed: 13 March 2017.

Thebault, Reis and Brittany Shammas. 2019. "Amber Guyger, police officer who shot a man to death in his apartment, found guilty of murder." *Washington Post*. Online: https://www.washingtonpost.com/nation/2019/10/01/amber-guyger-police-officer-who-shot-man-death-his-apartment-found-guilty-murder. Accessed: 1 October 2019.

Thielman, Frank. 1999. *The Law and the New Testament*. New York: Crossroad Publishing.

Thompson, James W. 2011. *Moral Formation According to Paul*. Grand Rapids: Baker Academic.

Thoreau, Henry David. 1960. *Walden and Civil Disobedience* (Orig pub 1854). Edited by Sherman Paul. Boston: Houghton Mifflin Company.

Thurow, Lester C. 1975. *Generating Inequality*. New York: Basic Books.

VanDuivendyk, Tim P. 2006. *The Unwanted Gift of Grief: A Ministry Approach*. New York: Haworth Press Inc.

Vanhoozer, Kevin J. 1998. *Is There Meaning in This Text? The Bible, The Reader, and the Morality of Literary Knowledge.* Grand Rapids: Zondervan.

Washington Post (WP) 2019. "Follow The Post's investigation of the opioid epidemic." Online: https://www.washingtonpost.com/national/2019/07/20/opioid-files/?arc404=true. Accessed: 24 September 2019.

Weithman, Paul. 2009. "Augustine's Political Philosophy" pages 234–252 of *The Cambridge Companion to Augustine.* Edited by Eleonore Stump and Norman Kretzmann. New York: Cambridge University Press.

Wells, David. 1998. *Losing Our Virtue: Why the Church Must Recover Its Moral Vision.* Grand Rapids: Eerdmans.

Wener-Fligner, Zach. 2015. "Every US company arguing for the Supreme Court to legalize same-sex marriage." March 10. Online: https://qz.com/359424/every-us-companyarguing-for-the-supreme-court-to-legalize-same-sex-marriage. Accessed 24 September 2019.

Wenham, Gordon J. 2012. *Psalms as Torah: Reading Biblical Song Ethically*. Grand Rapids: Baker Academic.

Whelan, Robbie. 2018. "Why Are People Fleeing Central America? A New Breed of Gangs Is Taking Over." *Wall Street Journal*. Online: https://www.wsj.com/articles/pay-or-die-extortion-economy-drives-latin-americas-murder-crisis-1541167619?mod=hp_lead_pos5. Accessed: 2 November 2018.

Weithman, Paul. 2009. "Augustine's Political Philosophy" pages 234–252 of *The Cambridge Companion to Augustine*. Edited by Eleonore Stump and Norman Kretzmann. New York: Cambridge University Press.

Williamson, Oliver. 1981. "The Modern Corporation: Origin, Evolution, Attributes." pp. 1537–1568 in *Journal of Economic Literature*. December.

Worden, J. William. 2009. *Grief Counseling and Grief Therapy: A Handbook for the Mental Health Practioner*. New York: Springer.

Zacharias, Ravi. 2011. "An Easter Meditation inspired by Counting Crows." Online: https://www.mhmcintyre.us/an-easter-meditation-inspired-by-counting-crows. Accessed: 16 April 2020.

SCRIPTURAL INDEX

OLD TESTAMENT

Genesis
1:1	x, 211, 109
1:2	28, 109
1–3	30
1:3	46, 95, 140
1:26	xi
1:26–27	118
1:27	41, 47, 95, 119, 109, 110
1:27	4
1:28	15, 141, 142, 109
1:31	101
2:8	109
2:15	109
2:17	210
2:24	14
3:6	109
3:16	229
3:18	229
3:24	109
4:1–8	93
9:11	92
11:1–4	141
11:7–9	142
12:1	44
12:1–3	13, 44, 96, 103
14:11–17	44
18:17–18	104
18:23	104
27:35	140

Exodus
3:2	126
3:4	126
3:5	126
3:6	43, 126
3:7	126
3:10	126
3:11	126
4:21	252
7:16	208
15:1	262
20:3	119
20:3	95
20:3–5	10
20:4–6	119
20: 7	140
20:7	99
20:8–11	184
20:12	35, 196
20:13	92
20:16	34
22:21–23	177
32:4	181
34:6	4, 43, 47, 106

Leviticus
11:45	190

Deuteronomy
5:12	178
5:15	179
5:17	92
6:4–5	123
6:5	xv, 11
24:1–3	110

Numbers
15:32–35	180

Joshua
1:8 73
4:5–7 263

1 Samuel
10:1 193
11:2 193

1 Kings
19:19–21 260

Psalms
1.2 73
8 110
8:2a 110
8:2b 110
19:1–2, 7–8 xiii
23 237
23:2 179
95:11 179
115:3–8 120
133:1 12

Proverbs
1:7 .... 34, 46

Isaiah
36:1 105

Ezekiel
34 237
34:2 237

Jonah
1:1–2 105
3:10, 4:1 106
4:2 106

Micah
6:8 32

NEW TESTAMENT
Matthew
4:1–11 22
4:6 23
4:7 23
4:19–20 43
5:14–16 .... 46, 96
5:16 214
5:17 54
5:21 .... 53, 92
5:21–22 53
5:23–24 93
5:24 92
5:25 149
5:27–28 48
5:29 193
5:30 193
6:9 166
6:10 4
7:15–16 191
8:26 246
9:9 8
10:32–33 8
10:38 116
11:28 178
12:8 178
19:3–9 110
19:18 92
22:21 152
22:36–40 .... 4, 11, 53, 96, 184
22:37 xv
25:14–15 75
25: 14–30 261
25:21 xvii
25:21,23 76
25:24–25 76
25:27 76
26:1–2 77

290 *Living in Christ*

(Matthew continued)
26:39 116
26:42 224
28:19 .... 44, 35
28:19–20 103

Mark
3:5 94
4:36–39 90
4:40 91
5:13 141
6:34 218
13:33 75

Luke
4:1–13 184
6:5 178
6:45 11
7:11–17 226
9:62 259
10:30–35 51
12:35 75
15 30
15:4–7 235
15:8–10 236
15:11–15 103
15:13–32 236

John
1:1–3 140
1:2–5 95
2 248
2:14–17 94
3:3 xvii
6 248
6:56 12
7:1 236
8:10–11 .... 238, 259

(John continued)
9 236
10 236
10:19 236
10:22 236
11:1–46 226
13:3–15 xix
13:5 18
14:3 44
15:1–5 80
15:2 193
15:16 7
15:26 69
17:1 166
21 248
21:18 24

Acts
1:16 166
2:1–4 142
2:38 xvii
2:44–45 166
4:36 87
8:1–3 152
21–22 153

Romans
1:21–23 100
5:3–4 .... 113, 117
8:22–23 110
12:1-2 145
13:1 152
13:9 92

1 Corinthians
1:2 12
1:10 166
5:11 35
6:19 184

(1 Corinthians continued)
7:12–14 15
7:16 15
9:24 xvii
15 211

2 Corinthians
5:19 162
7:10 223

Galatians
3:24 256
3:28 .... 55, 173, 228
5:16–24 42

Ephesians
4:20–24 194
4:22–24 43
4:30 191
5:1 .... 4, 42
6:1–4 55

Colossians
3:17 16

1 Thessalonians
1:4–5 245

1 Timothy
4:7 195

Hebrews
4:12 71
7 212
7:25 13
9:11–13 97

James
1:5 205
5:14 12

1 Peter
2:1–5 13

Revelation
1:8 56
11:18 106
19:9 14
22:2 179

ABOUT

*A*uthor Stephen W. Hiemstra lives in Centreville, Virginia with Maryam, his wife of more than thirty years. Together, they have three grown children.

Stephen worked as an economist for twenty-seven years in more than five federal agencies, where he published numerous government studies, magazine articles, and book reviews.

He wrote his first book, *A Christian Guide to Spirituality* in 2014. In 2015, he translated and published a Spanish edition, *Una Guía Cristiana a la Espiritualidad*. In 2016, he wrote a second book, *Life in Tension*, which also focuses on Christian spirituality. In 2017, he published a memoir, *Called Along the Way*. In 2018, he published a *Spiritual Trilogy* (an eBook compilation) and his first hardcover book, *Everyday Prayers for Everyday People*. In 2019, he published *Simple Faith*. *Living in Christ* (2020) is the fifth and final book in his Christian spirituality series.

Stephen has a Masters of Divinity (MDiv, 2013) from Gordon-Conwell Theological Seminary in Charlotte, North Carolina. His doctorate (PhD, 1985) is in agricultural economics from Michigan State. He studied in Puerto Rico and Germany, and speaks Spanish and German.

Correspond with Stephen at T2Pneuma@gmail.com or follow his blog at http://www.T2Pneuma.net.

www.ingramcontent.com/pod-product-compliance
Lightning Source LLC
Chambersburg PA
CBHW050206130526
44591CB00035B/2188